# KAILASH MANASAROVAR

CYCLE RIDES SOUL JOURNEYS

ANITA KARWAL
ANURITA RATHORE

Readomania

Readomania Publishing
A division of Kurious Kind Media Private Limited
466, DDA SFS Apartments, Pocket 1, Sector 22, Dwarka,
New Delhi – 110077
books.readomania.com
email: support@readomania.com
Facebook: facebook.com/iamreadomania
Twitter: twitter.com/iamreadomania

First Published in 2018 by Readomania



This book is based on true events.



ISBN: 978-93-858545-9-0

Typeset in Palatino Linotype by Shine Graphics
Printed in Delhi

# Readomania

India has traditionally been the land of storytellers and a lot of us have an inherent skill of creating good plots, good stories and good narrations. With a little encouragement and support, many more authors will be widely read and attain a place in the sun. This is the essence of *Readomania*—an initiative that nurtures emerging stars of the literary world.

It would not be an exaggeration to say that *Readomania* is the talent hunt in fiction. It goes a step beyond by not just identifying the talent but also nurturing it and showcasing it to the world. In the process, we have created a powerhouse of content.

*Readomania* has four principal interest areas—traditional print publishing, online library of short stories and poetry, literary events and products.

The print publishing works towards delivering good quality content to the readers. We publish good authors in meaningful anthologies, novels and works of narrative non-fiction. Our books stand out for their perspectives, the plots, the language and most importantly their ability to enrich lives.

Take a break, read something nice, write something beautiful. Read our books or visit us at www.readomania.com and enjoy a whole new world of literature.

*Dedicated to*

*Ankulanjana,*

*Janvi & Tanvi*

# About the Authors

## Anita Karwal

Anita likes to describe herself as 'an officer and a gentle mom'. She is a bureaucrat and belongs to the Indian Administrative Service. Her favourite pastimes include, reading, indulging her husband and kids, lording over the TV remote for watching sundry films and serials, and laughing at her own follies through the medium of columns that she has been writing for some English dailies. She has co-authored two books with Atul, her husband—*Think Everest* (2010) and *Everest – Same Path, Different Peak* (2016).

## Anurita Rathore

Anurita began her journey in journalism at 21 with *The Indian Express* and left day-to-day writing at the *Times of India*'s *Ahmedabad Mirror* after close to two illustrious decades. Some special features for *India Today* as well as exclusive interviews with celebrities for the web later, she took up offers to teach school and college students the fine art of writing and editing. An aesthete, Anurita enjoys listening to tales and experiences. She curates and infuses life in narratives, and believes stories must be told.

# Contents

*Take the lowest place,*
*and you shall reach the highest.*
*Hasten slowly,*
*and you shall soon arrive.*

*—Milarepa*

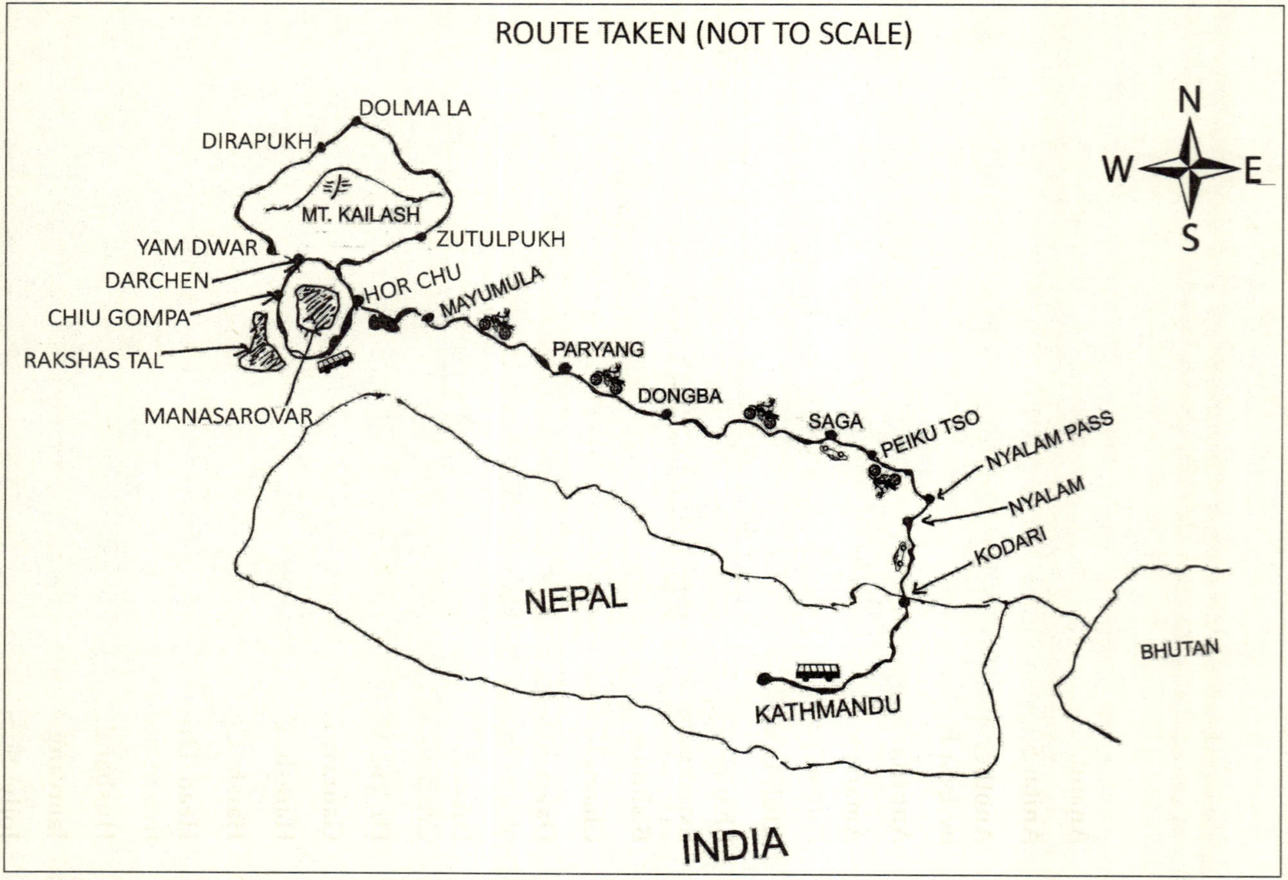

ROUTE TAKEN (NOT TO SCALE)

# Characters in the Book

**Anand:** Cyclist, doctor by profession

**Anita:** Support Group, bureaucrat, Atul's wife

**Another man from the other group:** Trekker from the group led by Isha Foundation

**Anurita:** Support Group, journalist, Kuldeep's wife

**Amar:** One of the three coordinators of the entire trip from Explore Himalaya based at Kathmandu

**Atul:** Cyclist, Police officer, Anita's husband

**Bharat:** One of the three coordinators of the entire trip from Explore Himalaya based at Kathmandu

**Bishnumaya:** Female porter at Kodari, Nepal

**Chameli:** Female porter at Kodari, Nepal

**Dawa:** The driver of the Land Cruiser in which the four members of the Support Group would ride together

**Drivers:** The Tibetan drivers; there were four drivers in four Land Cruisers and one in the truck

**Dr YK:** Well known practitioner of past life regression

**Gaurav:** Cyclist, has a bookstore, Supriya's husband

**Haresh:** Cyclist, entrepreneur

**Harsh:** Cyclist, orthopaedic surgeon, leader of the group

**Head Driver/Head D:** Head of the Tibetan drivers, who were five in number

**Husband:** An Indian officer, posted in Nepal

**Jamyang**: Guide in Tibet for the entire duration of the trip

**Jolly:** Supriya's pet dog who, as we write, is no more

**Kuldeep:** Support Group, in private sector, rugby player, Anurita's husband

**Kumaril**: Cyclist, entrepreneur

**Man from the other group:** Trekker from the group led by Isha Foundation

**Mauley:** Assistant from Explore Himalayas, Nepal

**Meh**: Tibetan female porter

**Muwyma:** Tibetan youth who rented a horse/pony to Anita

**Old man:** Septuagenarian who rented his horse/pony to Kumaril

**Pandey:** One of the three coordinators of the entire trip from Explore Himalaya, based at Kathmatndu

**Pemba**: Cook from Explore Himalayas, Nepal

**Popli:** Rajiv's last name is Popli, and he was often addressed as such

**Rajiv:** Cyclist, entrepreneur, innovator

**Sanjeeta:** Cyclist, environment consultant

**Sanjita:** Anita's cousin

**Satpal:** Cyclist, entrepreneur

**Sundari:** Female porter at Kodari, Nepal

**Sujata:** Female porter at Kodari, Nepal

**Supriya:** Support Group, owner of bookstore, Gaurav's wife

**Swati:** Support Group, homemaker

**Wife:** Wife of an Indian officer in Nepal; she hosted a wonderful dinner as a send-off for the group

**Woman from the other group:** A trekker from the group led by Isha Foundation

**Yalmin:** Tibetan female porter

# Introduction

***NOVATURIENT***

***No-va-too-ri-ent***

*(adj) Origin: Latin*

*Desiring or seeking powerful change in one's life;*
*It can be interpreted as the feeling that*
*pushes you to travel*

## From Anita's Desk

'What do you see?'

'A huge mountain of ice and snow, almost cylindrical in shape.'

'Climb up to the top of the mountain. Now what do you see?'

'Oh, well, the mountain is actually a hollow cylinder.'

'What do you look like?'

'I am about three years old, and I have long, flowing hair, white as snow.'

'Is there anyone else around?'

'Yes, I can see a fluorescent green torso of a man with emerald green dreadlocks, bobbing above me. He even has a half moon playfully circling his head.'

'What about the rest of his body?'

'The torso is all there is to him.'

'What are you doing right now?'

'I am kneeling at the edge of the peak of the mountain, hands folded in prayer.'

'Have you finished praying? What is happening now?'

'A flawlessly beautiful and extremely tall woman, almost as tall as a full-grown sequoia tree, dressed in red, has suddenly appeared.'

'What is she saying?'

'Nothing. She is smiling at me.'

'Now what is happening?'

'The woman has gently picked me up in her arms and is lovingly breastfeeding me.'

'How does it feel?'

'It feels divine, blissful, blessed.'

'What is the torso doing?'

'He is watching me feed with an indulgent look.'

'Now is the time for you to come back. Slowly absorb everything and remind yourself that you have to open your eyes.'

'Wait! The Greenman is sending his moon away from him.'

'Where has he sent it?'

'Ah! He is directing his moon into my forehead, at the point where my eyebrows meet.'

'What do you feel?'

'Complete.'

And then as I opened my eyes, I looked searchingly at Dr YK (name deliberately withheld, to maintain privacy), who had just taken me to my first birth on this earth, through past life regression. I began to cry uncontrollably, not knowing why I was doing so. Sanjita, my cousin, who I had insisted on accompanying me for this session, held my hands; I was shaking with unstoppable tears for a full fifteen minutes. The entire session had left me numb, shocked and serene, all at the same time. A few minutes later, several questions sprung in my head. I requested Dr YK to explain the whole experience to me.

He refused point blank. 'Nobody can interpret for you what you have been through. You have to find your own answers.'

It was the year 2007.

The Greenman, as I like to call the torso, would be in my thoughts constantly. It was then that I started looking for this mountain. Soon, I realised it resembled Mount Kailash. I had seen pictures of Mount Kailash earlier, but now that I could relate it to my experience, I felt drawn towards it. My consciousness had manifested nothing less than a divine mountain. My belief that we all come from divinity, was strengthened manifold by that one hypnotic yet powerful dip inside my deepest recesses. I am not a profoundly spiritual person, but I am attracted to the idea of an all-pervading consciousness, to the need to look within for a better understanding of the outside world, and to the interconnecting energy that resides in nature and its bounties.

The experience during the regression was so real for me that I developed this innate urge to sense the energy of Mount Kailash from close quarters, and kept looking for an opportunity. And when it came, even though in the form of a cycling expedition, and that too only up to Lake Manasarovar, I seized it. I knew that the energies of the universe desired it for me, and I was not going to let it slip away. It did not take much cajoling to convince the cyclists to extend the trip to include a *parikrama* of Mount Kailash.

There are several books that have been written on the journey to Mount Kailash and Lake Manasarovar by many a believer, trekker, writer, or traveller by addressing faith and prose to the scenic surroundings. This book, however, is more about friends, friendship, the bond between man and metal and the effect that a magical place has on your sensibilities. There is a thin line between humility and arrogance, and I would despise myself for crossing it; hence I will not draw any more comparisons. Because bicycles made this trip happen for me and Anurita, this book is written from the point of view of a bicycle. You will notice that the style is different, particularly when narrating conversations between friends. That is a measured move, just to lay emphasis on the fact that this story is narrated by a bicycle, which has a different take on life and its journeys, as compared to us humans.

I am not in the least familiar with bicycles. The one and only time I attempted to learn bicycling, that too at the ripe age of 35, I ended up with a torn meniscus, an arthoscopied knee and a hurt pride. Neither Anurita, nor I, have any idea of the machine that a bicycle is, or even the mechanics of its functioning. You will be able to discern that, largely because we are completely self-effacing about it, and also because our focus here is more on the interaction between man and nature through the medium of a bicycle.

A bicycle has taught me that just as its wheels return to the same point after every rotation, it is possible to take my awareness from the distractions of the world back to the same point each time, to the completeness and calmness within, to my soul. Through the Prologue and Epilogue, this is exactly what I have attempted to express—the two states that our mind and consciousness remain in—one, where the inside and outside are not connected, and two, where they are. So essentially, through this book, we hope to give you a glimpse of that completeness that lies deep within and is often revealed when man, bicycle and nature meet. Our success in achieving this tiny goal lies in your hands, literally!

## From Anurita's Desk

Certain experiences in life are strictly once in a lifetime. They could repeat, but they will never override that one time which either sealed the anticipation or altered an assumption surrounding it. This book, to put it upfront, is a translation of that feeling.

There's always a first time you hear a word, a name, before actually knowing what it is—person, place or something associated with either of the two. Kailash Manasarovar was written on a photograph framed and hung in the *pooja* room of my maternal grandmother and I remember seeing the majestic mountain as a little girl, covered in snow, with a distinguished look that spelt vast, enormous and magical, all at once. I gradually learnt and understood it to be the abode of Lord Shiva, the Supreme Power, and came to associate it with a pious energy that only spreads to cover and envelope those who seek it. In fact, even those who don't.

Years rolled by, I kept meeting people who spoke about this once-in-a-lifetime experience, about this *yatra* that is a calling, an undertaking of a strong mind that believes the magic is for real. This magic ought to be pursued, one heard many a time, but in the absence of any concrete plan to make it happen, time passed. Until an afternoon at a bookstore where I found myself standing with a group of cyclists, their better halves and some talk brewing about Kailash Manasarovar. Those words I first saw framed in that photograph walked into my life for real that day. A bunch of passionate riders planning to cycle it to the magical blue waters of the lake sounded too ambitious and fairytale-ish and yet, I believed it was possible. Why just possible, I could see myself there. Not on a cycle but around. That moment's thought, which I believe was a vision that manifested itself, is this book. I only remember turning to Anita, while the cyclists exchanged ideas and probabilities, saying, 'We could go, come back and write a book on this unique cycling expedition, a first of its kind ever.' Anita heard it like she already knew it. The thought took seed in our minds simultaneously and became the reason for us expressing joy at this undertaking. Somewhere, somehow, someone knew it would materialise. And it did. Everyday thereon was an experience in multiple energies and serendipitous happenings that often felt like a larger design working to make something happen. A plan was in place.

I rewound the childhood days to live through moments when my grandmothers or parents may have mentioned facts about Mount Kailash or Lake Manasarovar, its altitude and acceptance to human life. Bicycles, however, were never discussed or mentioned alongside. That's because there seemed no co-relation. But little had I known how bicycles would form the central idea of the expedition that would involve me at a later date, one I would participate in, and yet not cycle to. From tough terrains to delightful landscapes, it is owing to bicycles that we had enriching experiences. Their riders made the journey worthwhile. If not for their initiation, the thought of a book might perhaps not have taken seed. The very novelty watered the idea to narrate this story. And, it couldn't be told better than from the perspective of a cycle. The cycle is destiny's pick for a tell-all tale, from the journey's start to reaching the lap of Mount Kailash.

The premise of this book is a lot larger than what was envisaged. It talks about the journey, both inward and outward, of individuals and weaves in experiences that are life-changing. The cycle as narrator takes up the task and adventure of riding up to Manasarovar along with others like her. Those riding the cycles have first-time, first-hand experiences of life that when shared with people at large, could raise eyebrows, help connect with faith, absorb the everydayness of life and make everyone understand how everything done or not done, is part of a journey each mind and body undertakes. The five who chose not to cycle have experiences that are rich and varied, ranging from observations regarding the seen and unseen, to relationships between man and nature and how the two make for amazing stories. While the cyclists set out to achieve a goal and learnt much about life's little challenges or cherished accomplishments while paddling up, the non-cyclists found sublime joy in helping them achieve what they set out for—be it through encouraging words, helpful initiations or even basic human tenets of love and support for one another. And, of course, a lavish dose of humour in conversations!

This group of 14 enthusiasts are people with different ideas about sports, philosophies and life theories, but each one connects with the largeness and brightness of spirit required to undertake a trip as unique as this one. As you go through pages of this book, you will often feel you were along in the expedition. You will feel and realise how humans, by and large, are simple beings who have only joy at the core of their heart's desire. That it is machines and material gains that add complexities to life. Yet, with the right balance, these very machines and material gains can lead you to insurmountable joy. This expedition is testimony to the fact that machines can bring you to life, that they can give you a taste of heaven on earth. The key lies in how well you knit into the fabric of each other's lives.

Like the cycle made this book possible, I believe there is a 'cycle' in each of our lives that gets us going. Anita has been the cycle in writing this book. It is those wheels that ensured the ride was possible. A ride that I am sure, dear reader, you will enjoy and feel part of.

*The North face of Mount Kailash*
*Photo credit: Rajiv Popli*

*Resplendent Lake Manasarovar through prayer flags*

*Photo credit: Atul Karwal*

## *PROLOGUE*

### *Pro-log*

*(noun) Origin: Anglo-French, Latin and Greek*

*An introduction to a book in a unique fashion; curtain-raiser; a speech often in verse addressed to the audience of a play*

### *Outside me*

*There is a world*
*Where bliss and beauty*
*Unplug, unfurl*
*Where mountains rise*
*And lakes take birth*
*A jubilant sky*
*Meets a vivacious earth*
*Where spring and autumn*
*Together arrive*
*Where stone and water*
*Come alive*
*Where I often visit*
*To live a bit*
*To absorb it all*
*And merge with it.*

### *Inside me*

*There is a world*
*Where bliss and beauty*
*Unplug, unfurl*
*Where mountains rise*

*And lakes take birth*
*A jubilant sky*
*Meets a vivacious earth*
*Where spring and autumn*
*Together arrive*
*Where stone and water*
*Come alive*
*Where I often visit*
*In silence sit*
*To absorb it all*
*And merge with it.*

# 1

## *SATORI*

***Sa-toh-ree***

*(noun) Origin: Japanese*

*Sudden enlightenment and a state of consciousness attained by intuitive illumination representing the spiritual goal of Zen Buddhism*

We were 23 in number, nine of us and 14 of them. We were sturdy and they were fit. Silence defined us, while boisterousness did them. It is a curious fact but under the influence of our liberating togetherness, many a man and woman have gone off-track, and these 14 were about to be no exceptions! We are what desire is made of for spirited people, for they may have a bunch of very dear ones surrounding them but their desire for us would neither lessen in degree nor subside. Their list of hobbies will grow long but they will want to pursue us still. Luxury cars may steal their gaze but they will rest their eyes with fondness on us. Life may bring them several experiences but they will find us beside them till...till as long as memories are made and health smiles in adventure files.

Perish all thoughts of long-legged beauties, or six-pack studs, or anything else that has inebriated you in life, for we are far superior to them. We are the bicycle companions who befriend you once and then last forever. More loyal than your own body, mind or youth. More respectful than your boss, companion or relatives. More attractive than your car, motorbike or neighbour's spouse! You might forget how we strode our way through maddening traffic but what you will remember longer, are the rides we took amid serene environs, going up and down winding roads that led to places we explored together, those rides amid sturdy mountains and beautiful lakes.

So, I am a bicycle, but not just any bicycle; I am the chronicler of what you are holding in your hands. My narration might change the way you think about bicycles. If you never have thought about us before, I am about to prod you into changing that. We cycles (that's how I am fondly addressed by my loved ones) may have expressionless exteriors, but that does not mean we are deficient on the (e)motional scale. Our emotions are quite a reflection of the emotions of the cyclist riding us. I am incomplete without you, my rider; your riding makes me complete. When a cyclist and I travel, we are together and alone; it is then that we experience a range of sensations. So, while on this unique tour undertaken by cyclists, I decided to share their journey with the world. So that they know how man and machine come together, where for a change man adventures, and I, the bicycle, chronicles it all. There are no words between us and yet we are in sync; there is a connect that binds, thoughts that link. My cyclist and I journey along, creating little stories and experiences that introduce themselves to us.

You see me as metal and steel, tyre and tube, a beautiful creation of man, but I am not vain; this story is not about me. It is about those who move me, give me strength, with whom I come alive; it is about cyclists, who ride me, with or without a destination in mind. It is also about those who give strength and encouragement to those who give me strength; we call them the Support Group in this story. Furthermore, this story is about a mountain, a lake, a place, the wind, the clouds, the sky, the land, the colours and hues of nature...it is about everything that empowers us, the characters in this story and me.

The story I am about to embark on, unveiled right before my headlight. This story largely speaks of all that cycling in the mountains brings out in humans and is based on the sentiments of a cycle. Do you see as I do? Do you believe as I do? As members of this universe, we give each other strength, energy, life...which is how everything is interconnected. You, who is reading this, is connected to me, a cycle. Through me you are connected to the protagonists, and through them to the land and its people that figure in this story. Close your eyes, breathe in deeply, smile, imagine, be in the moment and feel the connections within this story and beyond. If it grips you, the sense of joy you shall feel permeating at your cellular level would be unparalleled. The emotion would connect you with the universe. Ephemeral, yet deep.

Even if you do not revel in romantic solitude and all that, cycling can be very liberating, especially when you pick a mountainous destination that is steeped in exquisiteness, sodden by the mercy of the weather gods and permeated with godliness. It is believed that extreme physical effort affords access to an altered state of consciousness. Athletic *satoris* are caused by the sheer exhaustion, thirst, hunger, risks, even loneliness that an athlete faces while indulging in extreme sports. The cyclists in this story picked Tibet and perhaps touched that state as they climbed Nyalam Pass, who knows. Though what I know is that an altered consciousness is not just the product of extreme sport, but also that of simply breathing in pristine and exquisite nature, slowly and steadily over a few days. And I cannot quite explain the reason why. I do not wish to apply intellect to this; its very application would ruin that moment and experience forever.

High up in the mountainous regions, not much human and other life can be supported. Hence, several aspects of human relationships that are the hallmarks of an urban or rural setting, for example, conflict, envy, greed, desire, materialism, fear, violence, inequality, etc. don't quite touch these 'high' places. That is the reason why monks and sages have preferred the height and the seclusion of mountains to deliberate on the finer aspects of human nature, the Self, love, generosity, spirituality, *et al*. Therefore, if not athletic *satori*, I knew we were all heading towards a nature and height-induced *satori*.

I speak and write from experience. You might label it wisdom, but if you tend to gather memories laced with information when you travel, I call it being sensible. I have noticed that most humans are predisposed to making elaborate arrangements for their travels and tours, including just the right apparel, accommodation, transport, intoxicants, even books to read, but when they reach the destination, they forget to absorb the place leisurely. The result is holiday completed, connection denied. Cycles, on the other hand, remain meditative and stationery when indoors, but when we hit the trails, nothing can stop us from remaining totally and absolutely in sync with the environs. We devour the beauty, imbibe the elements, soak up the history, sponge in the geography; we become osmotic! I hope I have made out a strong case for being the near-omniscient storyteller that I might appear to be as you turn the pages of this book.

So where do I begin? I could begin this story by describing in graphic detail to you the land that is Tibet. I could tell you in flowing prose about its mountains, rivers and forests; or perhaps wax eloquent about its people and habitations, its cultural vibrancy, its preference for the use of yaks to the dismay of us cycles. I could write at great length about the geological formations too. But I harbour this queer suspicion that your interest lies in human stories, and therefore, the possibility of you skipping such descriptions is high, if not certain. If I do touch these topics, I shall endeavour to be brief and factual.

Allow me instead to simply take you into the world of experiencing the uncertainties of a new place from atop a cycle, from inside Land Cruisers, from inside a tent, from the cold waters of a beautiful lake and from the exhausting climb around a mountain, all expressed in words that stem from deep recesses within. I begin with a *Koan* about cyclists. According to the *Merriam Webster Dictionary*, a *Koan* is 'a paradox to be meditated upon that is used to train Zen Buddhist monks to abandon ultimate dependence on reason and to force them into gaining sudden intuitive enlightenment'. As the story shall unfold, you will be able to draw similarities between the cyclists in the *Koan* and the cyclists in this story, and perhaps be able to see the reasons why dependence on reason is not always a reasonable idea! Regarding gaining sudden and intuitive enlightenment, my search is on, and I promise to educate you about it as soon as I reach that level. Meanwhile, I present the *Koan* to you (source: internet), followed gradually by the entire story of a cycling expedition to Lake Manasarovar and a trek around Mount Kailash.

> A Zen teacher saw five of his students return from the market, riding their bicycles. When they had dismounted, the teacher asked the students, 'Why are you riding your bicycles?'
>
> The first student replied, 'The bicycle is carrying this sack of potatoes. I am glad that I do not have to carry them on my back!' The teacher praised the student, saying, 'You are a smart boy. When you grow old, you will not walk hunched over, as I do.'
>
> The second student replied, 'I love to watch the trees and fields pass by as I roll down the path.' The teacher commended the student, 'Your eyes are open and you see the world.'

> The third student replied, 'When I ride my bicycle, I am content to chant, *nam myoho renge kyo.*' The teacher gave praise to the third student, 'Your mind will roll with the ease of a newly trued wheel.'
>
> The fourth student answered, 'Riding my bicycle, I live in harmony with all beings.' The teacher was pleased and said, 'You are riding on the golden path of non-harming.'
>
> The fifth student replied, 'I ride my bicycle to ride my bicycle.' The teacher went and sat at the feet of the fifth student, and said, 'I am your disciple.'

If you are expecting at this point, that I shall lapse into some kind of monologue about the deep philosophy behind this *Koan*, rest assured that I have full faith in your interpretative abilities and in your disgust for preaching. Allow me instead, at this juncture, to make you comprehend my intent about this book clearly. This book is neither a spiritual/moral discourse, nor a self-improvement handout. It is neither a thriller, a drama, a travelogue, nor is it a perfect piece of work written with the sole purpose of garnering awards. It is also not a lucid description of a foreign land, which can be of immense help and guidance in your travels there. I might not even end up conveying any useful titbit. I had once tried giving information about the workings of a cycle to some denizens, when I was rudely interrupted by one of them who reminded me in no uncertain terms that the internet is the answer to all questions in life these days. Therefore, all I am doing here is writing as I speak, and in the process attempting to enhance the joy that resides deep within each of us that adds to the richness of life.

The story begins with Anita and Anurita, and their idea of writing a book on a cycling expedition in Tibet that they were part of. Though the two women did not cycle, I have benefitted wholesomely from their daily banter. This book will, therefore, often seem as though written by them, and not by a cycle. Pray, do not let that fool you. That confusion is permitted to remain on purpose, for as I understand, it's a rare human who might give a cycle its due share of being heard. I will often stray from the story and draw your attention to snippets, written both in text and in verse. But then cycles are known to get 'carried away' very easily, hence, I seek your indulgence.

Sample this...

Anita has the habit of recalling stories from Indian mythology and I have acquired the expertise of lapping them up. I cannot but help recount the story of sage Dattatreya here, that Anita loves to tell and retell, and I am convinced that this has a bearing on this story.

Sage Dattatreya, also known as Parshuram's guru, is considered to be an incarnation of the trinity of Hindu gods: Brahma, Vishnu and Shiva. It is said that once the king of a neighbouring kingdom, King Yadu, happened to visit the *ashram* of the famous sages, Atri and his wife Anusuya, at Chitrakoot (this *ashram* exists even today). The couple had gone out, hence the king was welcomed by their son, Dattatreya. King Yadu was quick to notice the spontaneous reflection of the intrinsic beauty of the boy's soul on his blissful face. The King lost no time in questioning the boy about who his guru was. Dattatreya informed him calmly and most elegantly, that aside from his self, which resided deep within, he had twenty-four gurus outside. He learnt from them by simply observing them and internalising. He said his gurus were the earth, water, wind, fire, sky, moon, sun, flock of pigeons, a python, the ocean, moth, bumblebee, honeybee, elephant, deer, fish, a prostitute, a little bird, a child, a maiden, a snake, an arrowmaker, a spider and a worm. What remarkable gurus they were; I am not about to tell you what he learnt from each of them; you have your internet. But I will be doing Anita injustice if I do not give you a whiff of some of his learnings. He learnt,

- From the water: to cleanse whatever you touch, to provide life to your drinkers, and to keep flowing and keep moving to avoid stagnation.
- From the wind: to touch everything, whether flowers or thorns, to generously give them your essence, that is, freshness, but to never get attached to anything.
- From the fire: just like fire burns everything and produces a flame, to absorb everything that life gives, and transform it into a flame to enlighten life.
- From the sky/space: to be all-pervading, and to contain everything in yourself without getting affected by any of them.
- From the moon: that waxing and waning, rising and falling, losing and gaining, pleasure and pain are simply phases of life. While the phases may go on, one must maintain an unchanging core.
- From the sun: just as the sun saps water from everything, converts it into clouds, and then distributes it to all as rain, to collect knowledge from varied sources, transform it into practical wisdom and share it with one and all, with no discrimination.
- From a flock of pigeons: by watching one pigeon falling into a hunter's nest and the others following suit in a bid to rescue the one, he learnt that anything that springs from attachment, even if it is a positive reaction, can lead to bondage.
- From the ocean: to remain unmoved deep inside, even though multiple rivers might flow into it.

- From the fish: to not get caught by the baits offered in life.
- From a little bird: he watched as a little bird let go of the worm it had picked up, when larger birds pursued it and began pecking at it. He learnt the wisdom of renunciation for ensuring survival.
- From the spider: not to get entangled in the web of one's own making.

Dattatreya was, therefore, looking for and learning lessons from every walk of life, on every turn he took, every road he strode upon and everything he encountered. In a vast land like Tibet, with 14 cyclists in saddle, not a care in the world, and doing what I am best at, that is turning my wheels round and round, I did just that! Dear roads of Tibet, I learnt from you that however circuitous or winding, broken or stony, narrow or wide, steep or plain you maybe, one should simply rejoice in going somewhere, anywhere. Dear Lake Manasarovar, I learnt from you the sheer beauty of placidness. Revered Mount Kailash, you have taught me to rise majestically above all else that surrounds you!

Going ahead with the story, the idea of a cycle expedition took shape by charting a route, based on maps from the internet. And that is what lends the necessary thrill to this story. For the technologically challenged, there is this other-worldly charm about people who can interpret terrain maps from the confusion on their gadget screens. You are somehow sure that they are the only survivors of an alien intelligent race. You feel as if submitting yourself to their command is the only smart thing to do. But as we are about to discover, internet maps can ruin the calculations of a joyful ride, and yet make subsequent rides more joyful!

**I AM A CYCLE – KNOW ME**

Two wheels, both equal, tyred and tubed;
A wheel in the front, and one in the rear.
Each has a hub, and thirty-six spokes;
Contained in the hub, are the dynamo and gears.

To transmit power, there's a simple chain;
A certain tension though it must maintain.
Mounted on the handlebar, are the gears and brakes;
For stopping in the woods, or to speed attain.

A head tube, a seat tube, a down one and a top;
Each portion is connected to tubes galore.
Together they hold, each bit, every part;
Who would have thought mere tubes would score.

The saddle can be moved, up or down;
Its angle and position can also be changed.
Its height can be adjusted for affording comfort;
Such flexibility in life too, must be arranged.

The height of the handlebar, and its reach,
Is a matter that the cyclists personally decide
But the pedals must be so far from the saddle
That legs never straighten during the ride

Many other parts make a mountain bike
Each one is strong, but each one is light
The cycle is an extension of a rider's limbs
Together in flight, they each other ignite

So, affirm that your wheels are spinning straight
And check the chain for the presence of oil
Handlebar, brakes, tyre pressure check
Now head outdoors, and bond with the soil!

*The Sky above, the Earth below*

*Photo credit: Kuldeep Jadeja*

*Lake Manasarovar seen from the prayer wheels of Chiu Gompa*
*Photo credit: Atul Karwal*

# 2

---

*FERNWEH*

***Fi-urn-weeh***

*(noun) Origin: German*

*A longing for far off places, a desire to travel, wanderlust*

---

Two people riding in tandem on one bicycle is a rarity in the mountains. The rider in the front amidst his laboured breaths believes that he alone is responsible for moving the cycle, while the pillion at the back is convinced that had it not been for his companionship and joyful chatter, there would hardly be any motivation to ride. The peculiarity of singularity on cycles in the mountains, however, is a practiced avoidance of conversations with fellow cyclists, to save their lungs from declaring war on them. In our case too, we had singular riders on each of us.

On the other hand, two or more inside a four-wheeler, particularly two or more of the female species, share a camaraderie that is equitable and suited to the theme of this story especially as it is based on the word of mouth of two such damsels—Anita and Anurita. You put the two together anywhere, anytime, and be assured that a talkfest of the dimensions of a literary or theatre festival, shall unfold in minutes. With the two there is nothing that stays within hidden depths as indescribable emotions; everything is elucidated, illustrated and transmitted to all within audible range with the kind of detailing that might put a ten-pixel camera to shame. All that emanates from me here is nothing but their chatter taking possession of me—at times idle, at times philosophical, but mostly graphic, tickled and peppy.

Interestingly, this trip was neither Anita nor Anurita's idea. Although Anurita is capable of writing extensive journalistic pieces, and Anita of making copious notes on bureaucratic files, and though both are known to multi-task to levels of godliness or at least creating such an illusion, when tasked with any outdoor activity, the duo is enthusiastic, but often shaky. They are, in fact, famous for making 500 New Year resolutions every month about their fitness goals and not following them. They are also adept at planning every other day in much detail for visiting gyms and power yoga classes in search of their midriffs, and developing amnesia about it soon after. However, egged on by their significant others, occasionally they do end up adding variety-of-the-adventure-kind to their lives.

Anita, Atul's wife, mother of two grown-up daughters, is a bureaucrat who believes that her foray into motherhood and wifehood are nothing short of acts of bravery. After watching the movie *Batman*, she remains most impressed to date with one dialogue of the Joker, 'Why so serious?' And that dialogue essentially sums up how she likes to lead her life. She is fragile of limb, but resilient of will. She is barely 5 feet 2 inches tall, puny, short-haired, and always clad somewhat business like. She is also acclaimed for the inexplicable mental confusion that grips her to the point of insanity when faced with anything that requires the combined attention of her limbs and other faculties, and that includes driving or riding bicycles. Yet, she has been caught rappelling down 10-12 storied buildings to her own amazement, or going trekking on some tiny hill entirely against the wishes of her groaning muscles, or if inspired enough by the taunts of her kids, she has even jumped into a friendly sea for scuba-diving!

Anurita, tall, slim and pretty, with brown eyes that twinkle ever so often, is fortunate to have been bestowed naturally and genetically with good health and sumptuous energy, therefore not content with the workout that being a journalist provides, she nurtures a travel bug. And I would give up a cool ride any day just to watch her light brown tresses blow in the wind. Anurita is a journalist and an art connoisseur, well known for her stories based on real life. This trip was her initiation into the big world of extreme adventure—the kind where you go without a proper bath for days, one where luxuries are boxed aside for future reference. She is married to Kuldeep, and her faith in him, next only to God, is unshakeable. She believes it is the Supreme Power that chalks out our lives and at the same time, she strongly feels we ought to take charge of our life, to lead it up to where we want to go.

Despite their moderate attempts at acquiring a taste for the outdoors, generally speaking, I like to categorise Anita and Anurita under 'humanity of the stationary kind'. Of the three levels of existence—physical, verbal and mental—physical is not exactly their cup of *masala* tea. This background was necessary to stress upon the fact that nothing they had ever done really prepared them for the cycling-cum-trekking trip to Lake Manasarovar and the sacred Mount Kailash, both located in Tibet, China.

The cycling expedition was an idea that struck Harsh and Gaurav. Harsh, about 6 feet tall, if not more, bespectacled, fit and handsome in a very doctor sort of way (you know the kindly, happy and intelligent sort of doctors that you like to visit routinely only if to discuss the possibility of you falling sick in some unknown future), is an orthopaedic surgeon.

Gaurav, taller and lankier than Harsh, though as bespectacled as him, keeps his hair so closely cropped, that the combination of his moustache, hairstyle and carriage give him the demeanour of a service personnel that has often sent policemen on the street scurrying to salute him. He is credited with the introduction of the delights of rummaging through shelves upon shelves of books, and reading and buying them, to a bookstore-starved urban populace.

Harsh was the national swimming champion and the local champ in tennis, badminton and gymnastics in his youth. He later took to running and cycling, immersed himself in both, and loved it. But some years ago, due to a medical condition in his ankle which could have eventually led to joint replacement in some future universe if not heeded to, he had to stop running. It is not an easy matter to perturb Harsh, whatever outrageous potshots luck takes at him. In such a situation, he can be counted upon to change the course of his life with the calmness of the water that lies at the bottom of an ocean. Harsh decided to create his own little success story. That is when he began to cycle, and the rest is psychology! To put it mildly, the cycle and he became inseparable. Harsh tends to develop an emotional relationship with every aspect of sport he indulges in. And thus, he ended up with in-depth knowledge of every part of the cycle and its functioning. A tiny sound anywhere in the cycle, and he is known to transfer his gaze, scrutiny and repairing skills to the exact spot. His cycle-restoration abilities are akin to his famous surgical skills for joint restoration, both in precision and efficiency. I should know, for I was Harsh's companion during this expedition.

Gaurav began running about 15 years ago for fitness. He had cycled, but up to high school and only for fun. He belongs to that determined breed, who, feeling that legs keep better if constantly on the run, devoted himself to the task of overdoing his part. Soon enough he tore a cartilage and was advised to see a good doctor. That is how he met Harsh, way back in 2003. Harsh did his doctor bit, but eager for company, the cyclist in him couldn't help but enrol Gaurav for daily cycling. Since that day Gaurav maintains two sets of friends—those who cycle with him, and those who run with him. Atul falls in the common portion of his Venn diagram. The book business is now third priority. Supriya, the wife, is alright with it. She has Jolly. But we shall come to that a little later. Gaurav has an unmatched ability to order people around, particularly about being on time. A man of sharp witty words, his wit is often misunderstood as sarcasm. This came in handy ever so often.

It was August 2012. Harsh and Gaurav, the founders of Ahmedabad Bicycling Club, were tired of the same cycling routine day after day.

**Harsh:** I want to ride to a new place. Even the stray dogs recognise me now!

**Gaurav:** How can you be so sure of that?

**Harsh:** Well, they have stopped barking when I cycle past.

**Gaurav:** Now that is a serious matter.

**Harsh:** I feel I am going on and on in a loop now. My riding path stagnates, I stagnate.

**Gaurav:** Explanation accepted. Next line of thought please!

**Harsh:** We have already done Manali-Leh-Khardungla on cycles last year. Any ideas?

**Gaurav:** Abroad.

**Harsh:** Abroad? Flat ground or undulating?

**Gaurav:** Can cycle, will cycle anywhere.

**Harsh:** I am thinking an ethereal place like Manasarovar, Tibet.

**Gaurav:** I am game. When?

**Harsh:** What do you mean when? It takes a lot of planning to go on a cycling expedition of this kind.

**Gaurav:** Then plan, and let me know the schedule by tomorrow.

**Harsh:** Gaurav, you are such a tyrant! You know, in the dead of the night, when little babies cry, their moms tell them, 'Baby go to sleep, or Gaurav will come and demand the plan for the rest of your life!'

**Gaurav:** I suppose I am expected to fly into a rage at this point!

The idea was firmed up somewhere in March that year for an August trip. Initially, for no particular reason, it was a trip planned and meant only for Harsh and Gaurav. But when they decided to add a few friends from the Ahmedabad Bicycling Club (ABC), the trickle of willing people began to show symptoms of expanding into a flood in no time. Harsh being Harsh, knew that he had a calendar full of sleepless nights ahead, if the numbers went out of hand. 'Fourteen, and no more please,' was his emphatic request. The request was respected and therefore adhered to. The 14 who thus got together by some play of fate and enthusiasm, may not ever be one on the politics of the nation, or the best place to eat out, or some such crucial matter, however, they were unanimous over choosing Harsh as the Tour Leader. Harsh as the Tour Leader was, well, more detailed than the detailing of the parts inside a rocket about to take off for Mars. He took care of everything and nothing missed his keen, meticulous approach. There wasn't a day when he was not either exchanging emails with Explore Himalayas, their tour agency in Nepal, or telling them what to do, how to do, or planning the pre-expedition training of the cyclists, or studying the route of the expedition on Google maps, and so on.

The body is the medium for attaining anything in life, and Harsh knew this better than most others, what with his orthopaedic knowledge of over 650 muscles and 206 bones! He ensured that the cyclists got used to the grind of cycling long distances, and had enough hill training (Mount Abu was chosen for this). The hill practice sessions were arranged on weekends, while the routine training of getting used to long hours of cycling was undertaken on weekdays, early in the morning, much before sunrise, on the roads of Ahmedabad city. When the cyclists would emerge every other day on the streets of the city to practice, they would often be cheered by spectators, less for their show of might, and more for the pleasure and conscientious efforts, writ large on their faces.

And thus, the journey of a thousand miles began with the diminished rapture of dogs that had stopped barking after a cyclist!

# 3

***ENSEMBLE***

***On-som-bl***

*(noun) Origin: French*

*A group of people or things; that make up a complete unit, such as musicians in a performance*

They were a strange mix of people, the expedition members. There were 14 of them: eight who were acclaimed cyclists of the ABC; one who would join them from Delhi (Rajiv); four who knew cycling but preferred not to; and one, that is, Anita, who couldn't cycle to save her life!

Harsh was the unanimous and obvious choice as leader of the group, also for the reason that no one else was as prepared for hurling himself into planning, at breakneck speed that is.

Besides Harsh and Gaurav, the other seven cyclists included Atul, Haresh, Satpal, Kumaril, Anand, Sanjeeta and Rajiv. Haresh is tall and strong and looks exactly like a dashing entrepreneur which he also happens to be. One of the most helpful members of the group, he has a soft but firm approach—to people and things. Kumaril, too, is a businessman whose chief characteristic is a comical glint in the eyes that is more than apparent behind his spectacles; he is blessed with a sturdy body and an entertaining mind. Atul is a cop and an Everester (he scaled Mount Everest in May 2008, as a member of the first Indian Police Everest Expedition), who is ready to try out any sport as long as it involves extreme effort. His tall, fair and handsome looks are a cause for heads, mostly belonging to the opposite gender, to turn, and turn acutely. Anand is a doctor, stocky and fit, strong and silent, still recovering from a severe paralytic attack. Rajiv, who fitted into the 'acclaimed cyclist' category by his sheer insistence on joining the group as a cyclist despite his 'uncycled' fitness, is such a pleasant man that when you have said that of him, you have said everything. He is from the corporate world and can go to the end of the earth to click a good photograph. Sanjeeta, a sporty woman, is a mountaineer and a marathon runner and loves to make repeated attempts to challenge her capacity. With the exception of Kuldeep and Anurita (who are in their thirties), all the cyclists and members of the Support Group were either in their late forties or early fifties, whatever else their claims maybe.

Initially it was only eight members of ABC and Rajiv who were participating. But, when the idea extended to doing a *'parikrama'* (circumambulation) of Mount Kailash as part of the cycling tour, then Supriya (Gaurav's wife and business boss), Swati (Swati's husband is Supriya's brother), Kuldeep, Anurita (Kuldeep's significant other) and Anita (Atul's better half), joined in and promptly designated themselves as 'Support Group'.

Interestingly, these 14 did not begin as friends, at best they were acquaintances. It was during the expedition-trip that lasting friendships developed. Not all qualify for the gifted conversationalist category either. In fact, some like Satpal, Anand, Haresh or Sanjeeta seldom spoke unless spoken to, and any disposition that they might have had towards small talk would be arrested by the boisterousness of the rest in the group. It was during the trip that Anita and Anurita would often tear themselves away from the engaging beauty of Tibet, in an attempt to draw the cyclists into a technical conversation about the joys and perils of cycling. It was my stroke of luck as I stood outside the door listening in, and for this I adore them. Through these conversations I came to understand how man and machine can have a deep and loving relationship as long as there is some bit of nature thrown in.

**Anita:** I'm curious. As cyclists what would you rate your strength and weakness as?

**Harsh:** My strength—consistency on the plains; my weakness—the climbs.

**Anita:** Plains? In Tibet? Hmm. What were you thinking?

**Harsh:** With all the organising to consider, I really wasn't thinking. But seriously, I have done Manali-Leh-Khardungla on cycle. There I had once hit a wall and collapsed only to discover I am not too good with climbs.

**Anurita:** So, how will you tackle the climbs here?

**Harsh:** With high spirits I'm sure, for I look forward to securing 'bragging rights' towards the tour's end.

**Gaurav:** I am better than him at climbing, I've gorilla legs. But I am unable to deviate from a plan; so am physically flexible, but mentally not quite.

**Anita:** Do you need to be a runner or sprinter to be able to do well at climbing hills on a cycle?

**Gaurav:** Well, a sprinter should do well for the first 30–40 km at least owing to good leg muscles. Beyond that is really a test.

**Harsh:** Weight, you see, is the real issue with both—the cycle and the cyclist. A sturdier and heavier cycle may be more stable, but also a lot more difficult to ride uphill. The Tour de France guys have cycles weighing not more than 7 kg, ours are close to 12–13 kg. Likewise, the heavier the cyclist, the heavier is the weight he has to carry.

**Rajiv:** True, and a lighter or thinner cyclist may not have enough muscle to ride.

**Anita:** It seems like such a precarious balance and struggle for the right weight. The story of my life! What about the rest of you? Strengths and weaknesses?

**Atul:** I gain energy over long distances and am not too sure how I will do on the hills as I manage to goof up on pacing. I know I cannot maintain a high pace for too long but sometimes my enthusiasm gets the better of me!

**Anurita:** And why do you cycle, Atul? I'm sure it is beyond just fitness and fun.

**Atul:** Because I will do anything that's an outdoor activity. I like to test my limits. I evolve a bit more each time I handle my fears and exert beyond my capacity. I feel very alive and vibrant when I am in the hills. I am not the silent types when I ride. I yell, I laugh, I cajole, I cheer, and I am quite a child! What really irritates many is when I stop every few metres to take photographs. Can't help it, I feel I need to capture all forms of natural beauty for posterity.

**Anita:** Okay Atul, so what do you want to be when you grow up?

**Atul:** What gives you the impression I will ever grow up? I am Forever 21!

**Gaurav:** I think you are raising not two, but three kids, Anita.

**Atul:** Hey, don't even get me started on who is more of a kid!

**Anurita:** At times we all are! Alright, let's turn to Rajiv... how are you here? You joined in from Delhi, and knew nobody except Atul in this group.

**Rajiv:** Well, my desire for trying out new things has overtaken the practical reality that this indeed is the first time I shall be cycling such a crazy distance over an even crazier landscape. When outdoors, I lose any sense of urgency, and merge with the surroundings. I stop making efforts to reach anywhere, almost as if the destination shall present itself. And then outdoor activity, especially in the hills, is a high.

**Anurita:** And Satpal, you've always been a cyclist, right?

**Satpal:** You know how I started? I bought a cycle for my teenage son but since he was studying in a residential school in Dalhousie, the cycle would lie unattended till the day I decided to get on it and cycle from home to the Gurudwara. Thereon, it was routine. As I gained stamina, I heard about ABC and joined them, and here I am. I think I do well in plains, but I do know I am a really slow climber!

**Anurita:** Sanjeeta, you are the only woman cyclist in this group. That makes you feel a wee bit special, doesn't it?

**Sanjeeta:** I love all forms of sports and that's my strength. The sheer adventure and accompanying excitement of the Manali-Leh-Khardungla (MLK) cycling expedition inspired me enough to join ABC. Cycling for me is means to unconditional freedom and independence. And woman or not, this group would not have let me join this trip had I not been tested and found worthy!

**Anita:** It's not without reason that we ladies cheer you the loudest. Haresh, why do you cycle?

**Haresh:** I feel very energetic and fresh in doing so. It is like meditation for me. I never wire myself up to music when cycling. No external and artificial distractions for me. I just love listening to the sounds of nature and experiencing those temporary, beautiful moments completely.

**Anurita:** And Anand, I believe you have been through plenty of physical hardships before you became a cyclist. But your resolve to cycle remains strong. . . .

**AN ODE TO AN EXPEDITION CYCLIST**

Scorching sun
Wind in hair
Dripping sweat
Fully aware

My hands, my feet,
My eyes, my mind,
The pedal, the path,
And the handle aligned

Crossing lakes
Hills and trees
Abandoning thought
My spirit free

Bumpy roads
I might get hurt
But man and machine
Endlessly flirt

I ride, I ride
I feel the thrill
While gliding down
A rolling hill

Exploding lungs
On a climb uphill
But beckoning clouds
Take me higher still

Muscles sore
Bones that ache
A sudden turn
Oh, hit the brakes

It does not matter
How fast, how far
Birds in flight
That's who we are

Above the earth
Beneath the sky
In mindful mirth
My cycle and I.

**Anand:** I was a hemiplegic a few years back. I think I brought it upon myself by leading a careless life! Once I recovered substantially I got into a fitness regimen. I heard of ABC, got inspired and started cycling on my own, simply to see if I would fit their bill. In 20 days I decided to join them.

**Harsh:** His left hand was struck by paralysis thrice; it is still slightly affected and yet he is here! What an amazing spirit!

**Gaurav:** We call him the Lance Armstrong of ABC! Minus the doping, of course!

**Anita:** Why did you choose cycling over other sport?

**Anand:** For one, I like the silence that surrounds me when I cycle. Cycling does away with the need to chat, to make small conversation, or participate in a discussion simply to be noticed. And two, it de-stresses me big time.

**Haresh:** Speech, you see, is really a reflection of one's mind. When you are cycling in silence, it is possible to contemplate upon the connection between our speech and our mind.

**Anurita:** In fact, there is an internal dialogue, a silent one, and that puts a lot of things in perspective.

**Anita:** My internal dialogue is like a full-fledged conference going on. I have tried million times to silence it. But I am told by wise people, that being the originator and creator of my speech, and hence my thoughts, I must learn to bring peace to my tongue first to quieten the mind. But that does not work for me. I am the one who invented chatting, you see!

**Anurita:** Cycling on a quiet stretch helps to bring the peace you talk about. I loved cycling when in school; I wonder why I never continued my association with the machine. It was enjoyable to cycle, observe life and people around and generally go by free-spiritedly. Even for those of us who enjoy the company of people and large crowds, the act of cycling that alienates you with everything and everyone else is very fulfilling and, well, necessary. On quiet streets, it is the 'me' time that is deeply meditative and relaxing. On crazy roads with overflowing traffic, I'm sure it is the reverse! Alright, so Kumaril, any inner peace in the offing for you?

**Kumaril:** My strength is my resolve to finish the task each day, even if I am exhausted. And when I do finish, I enjoy the ride even more the next day, in the next stretch. I never thought of it this way earlier, but perhaps the excitement of finishing a tough ride is equivalent to inner peace for me.

**Gaurav:** Tell them what you did on the TFN[1] tour.

---

[1] Tour of Nilgirs, which spans over 1,000 km, through three wildlife sanctuaries of South India—Bandipur in Karnataka, Waynad in Kerala and Mudumalai in Tamil Nadu.

**Kumaril:** Well, we were about to complete the toughest 24 km stretch of the tour. In the excitement of it all, I started chatting with my co-rider and unknowingly applied brakes on the front wheel of my cycle.

**Anurita:** And?

**Kumaril:** I fell flat on my face!

**Harsh:** And it needed seven stitches on his face to make him look like a human being again!

**Gaurav:** Now you tell us, why you joined us, especially you Anita, despite not knowing how to cycle.

**Anita:** I think we all need someone who introduces an element of adventure in our lives. My 'someone' is home-grown—Atul. Every small or big outdoor activity we have done together has had its unique moments. At least that's what I remember about them. Perhaps, I am here for adding to my kitty of unique moments and memories, or maybe I am here to cater to my spiritual side. Either way, I am happy to be here.

**Supriya:** I joined in because I had no other option once I made a commitment. Let's go and see what this journey unfolds.

**Swati:** The thrill and effort of the outdoors is what draws me.

**Anita:** And Anurita, you are a strong believer in God. Is that your calling?

**Anurita:** For me God is awareness of a Higher Being, and my calling is the recognition of that awareness. Graduating from the comforts of home to being in the lap of the mountains helps assess the true meaning of life and its worth. There's an alternative energy that you experience when you decide on undertaking the improbable. It is as if several voices within are hooting for your decision even before you have reached out to act upon it. And so, knowing you can do it is important. Believing you will do it, even more so. And I am a believer.

**Anita:** And you. Kuldeep, what prompted you to join?

**Kuldeep:** I am up for anything sporty. I love outdoors and if it is Manasarovar, you've got to go for it. Since I don't cycle regularly, I decided against it for lack of practice. But I love the outdoors in any format! Luxuries and joys that involve satiating desires can never compete with joys that involve desiring the unknown. May be this was fated. Look, I have a tattoo on my left arm that reads '*Om Mani Padme Hum*'. This was etched seven years ago!

*While 12 of the group pose, two are busy behind the camera*

*Photo credit: Satpal Singh Chhabda*

*The giggly foursome*

*Photo credit: Kuldeep Jadeja*

# 4

**_HYGGE_**

**_Hue-gah_**

*(noun) Origin: Danish*

*The cosy feeling you get while you are enjoying good things in life with friends*

The women in this story could not help being fascinated. There is a relaxed and kindly air that they had come to associate with any form of vacationing. But when it came to holidaying in the outdoors, how could they not be captivated by the idea to the point of an aching heart and curious mind! Without a quibble or doubt, all five members of the Support Group felt that this trip was going to agree with them. All their lives they had spent in dealing with yearnings to visit untouched nature. And here it was—with a vivacity and just that much element of adventure and friendship, as if scripted for them.

Supriya, Swati, Anita, Kuldeep and Anurita, who formed the Support Group, joined in to support the cyclists in their expedition and simultaneously contemplate on the vastness and the completeness that is Tibet. As I said before, they were not friends to begin with, but whatever was the pre-planned act of the universe that brought them together, it just was meant to be. It was the beginning of a deep and delightful bond. Anita and Anurita would often discuss at the end of each day, while standing and leaning against one of us, that there was something in it written for each of them on this trip. You will see towards the end that each absorbed the mountain and the lake in an experience that was exclusive to them.

Initially, Supriya, Gaurav's wife, a sworn vegan, therefore bony thin, but sturdier than many, had refused to even consider joining a trip that required even one night away from home and Jolly, her pet dog. It was only after her lawyer daughter agreed to take leave from work to take care of Jolly in her absence that Supriya agreed to join. Supriya, of the-chilled-out-attitude fame, is a dusky beauty who has never suffered from poverty of language when it comes to communicating with animals. Her love for animals (irrespective of species, size, looks or ferocity) had the others donating their precious packed food once too often on the trip to every stray dog, who looked at them with melting eyes and salivating tongue.

Swati has dark and beautiful kohl-lined eyes, a face that is small, shining and charming, with lips that appear to be smiling at all times, good or bad. The women were fascinated when they discovered that the perfectly lined black kohl on her upper eyelids was, in fact, a tattoo. This is one adventure-loving housewife! She is a toughie who had played badminton at state and national levels before she got married. A homemaker, she is mother to two sons and likes living life on her own terms, which includes intense focus on fitness, badminton and music. She would have made a good Nancy Drew or Hermione as far as the group was concerned, particularly the ladies. You shall see why, though a bit later.

Kuldeep, a tall, lean and handsome young man of royal bearings from the corporate world, is a person with delightful linguistic capabilities. He is prone to joyousness and believes in the simplicity of life. He could see through a camera what others often missed with their plain sight. Kuldeep, whose likeness to a Greek god is startling in almost all respects except for being a human, became the biggest support for the Support Group. His kindness and readiness to help everyone in whatever they required, left behind a certain devoted flock of damsels for sure.

The girls in the Support Group prepared for this expedition-trip with ridiculous levels of intelligent planning.

**Anurita:** I do hope we will get to bathe on the expedition days?

**Swati:** Just carry wet wipes. Use it to semi-bathe yourself.

**Anurita:** No clean washrooms, no set-up whatsoever?

**Anita:** The entire landscape shall be our washroom. You can select your spot, and mark your territory!

**Anurita**: Goodness! This surely is an adventure of the unforeseen kind.

**Swati**: How many changes of clothes do you think we should carry?

**Anita:** One that you are wearing, and two more.

**Anurita:** Really! You mean either washing or wearing the same clothes days on end? And then, the cold!

**Anita:** Except for inner wear, we will not need to change for days together.

**Supriya:** So stinking is not an option!

**Anurita:** Then we might as well carry disposable inner wear.

**Anita:** Wow! Never heard of this.

**Anurita:** Oh yes, you get them.

**Anita:** One learns.

**Swati:** And how!

**Anurita:** Ah! This trip shall be an exercise in knowledge expansion. There is so much I am learning from just talking to you people. You are like my personalised internet service!

Incidentally, Sanjeeta would not get to learn what the rest of the women would through their giggly conversations, due to her preoccupation with unexciting meetings with the cyclists.

**Supriya:** Why did you not ever learn cycling, Anita?

**Anita:** Because of the inherent dangers involved. Even though danger is a rarity in my life, I never think twice before running away from it!

**Swati:** (More than a little bemused) Dangers in cycling, how?

**Anita:** Of balancing, you see. And falling for not being able to do that!

**Anurita:** Ha ha. Looks like we will be learning all of life's elusive lessons in this one trip!

# 5

***FUGLEMAN***

***Few-gle-man***

*(noun) Origin: German*

*A leader or a manager;*

*A trained soldier posted in front of a line of soldiers at drill to serve as a model in their exercises*

Harsh, as expedition leader, prepared like he was preparing for the launch of a space satellite. His medical practice kept him busy and he did everything else in the little spare time he had. But, whatever it be, you simply have to plant the possibility of an idea into his head, and then let nature take over.

In dizzying succession, he can dish out plans for everything; in this case he had detailed plans for schedule, logistics, even the kind and make of cycles/vehicles/camping and other equipment required. For example, please see the specifications of cycles. You might notice that I am of immaculate breeding.

There was a plan for everything: day-wise plans, movement plans, even menu plans for the three meals every day. Just a hint of a potential crisis is capable of buoying his spirits. Why else would one go to the extent of preparing a near-perfect Level of Services document and give it to the tour operator (and to each one in the group)? While he prepared fervently, the rest of the members sat back and relaxed in the satisfaction of the knowledge that they were perhaps a strange, but unquestionably wonderful group, for being able to trust so completely in their group leader.

**EXTREME PLANNING BY HARSH:**

**Make of the bicycles to be supplied by the tour agency:**

a. Trek
b. Specs
    i. Front lockable jumpers
    ii. Sleek tires (not thicker than 32 mm)
    iii. Bike Name: Trek—6000—6 series
    iv. Bike size: 19.5" to 21.5"
    v. Frame Quality: Alpha SLR Aluminum
    vi. Front Suspension: Rock shox
    vii. Crank Size: Shimano 44-32-22
    viii. Front & Rear Derailleur: Shimano Deore
    ix. Sifter Front & Rear 2 finger: Shimano Deore
    x. Wheel Size: 26"
    xi. Brake System: Both mechanical Avid Disk Brake
    xii. Free Wheel: Cassette 11-32 T
c. Adjustable seat post

The tour agency may not have started out by perceiving the world as Harsh did, but they ended up much educated, enlightened, in admiration, and on the same page as him. The entire set of email discussions between Harsh and them when put together, was a scholarly volume of a-place-for-everything-and-everything-in-its-place proportions, containing detailed action plans for the group's permits, visas, safety, logistics, personnel for assistance, vehicles for the tour, tents and the like.

Just as Harsh and the agency were coming to the significant conclusion that nothing, absolutely nothing could go wrong with this trip, they received information that Tibetan group visa does not permit splitting the group or even a slight deviation from the route, and that there can be serious consequences for doing so. Truth be told, the 14 members did have their initial apprehensions on whether this cycling expedition was a good idea at all. But public memory is short, and they were a rather large group of public, hence, memory was shorter still. After a tiny but affectionate discussion on how they might end up languishing in Chinese jails, they forgot all about it. Some question-answers, some silly laughter, and they carried on.

I would maintain a close watch out, for my two ladies and their ponderings on the conversations in the group, just as a mother-in-law would on her daughter-in-law's cooking, cleaning and parenting skills. In a meeting called a few days prior to the date of departure, I came to know that the following chat took place:

**Cyclist:** (On phone) What time should I be there for the meeting?

**Gaurav:** You have been informed on email and SMS.

**Cyclist:** But I have misplaced those messages.

**Gaurav:** ABC time, 8 pm; Gaurav time, 7.45 pm!

I am sure the cyclist could almost sense over the phone, the intense stare he may have received from Gaurav on the other side...you know the kind your teenager kids give when they are told they cannot buy a new dress every week only because it is available online!

What I have heard about the meeting and the elaborate discussions on the care they were taking for packing up for the expedition, could impress any cycle worth its wheels. Of course, with Gaurav and Atul in the meeting, seriousness always got the shove by light-hearted repartees.

**Harsh:** I hope all of you have got the red T-shirts that I got customised for our expedition.

**Anurita:** Oh yes! But you have issued me an S size T-shirt and I am wondering if I will fit into it.

**Gaurav:** You have four days. Lose 4 kg!

**Harsh:** Be comfortable. Will issue you an M size.

**Haresh:** There are so many things we need to pack for cycling. It is confusing, especially because we continue to do our cycling practice every day. I use the stuff and don't know if I will remember to pack it back.

**Harsh:** Follow my system. I have placed all my cycling stuff on an extra bed at home. When I go cycling, whatever I pick from there, is carefully returned and placed back at the same place.

**Atul:** Yes Haresh, do that. In fact, why don't you maintain a register of equipment? Make entries everyday about what you have issued to yourself. You know, the best part is that you can refuse to issue some stuff to yourself!

**Harsh:** Okay now. I have issued detailed instructions on the essentials of packing for such a trip. And don't forget to carry petroleum jelly. You will need to apply it on your cycling shorts before wearing them, so that your skin does not chafe.

**Atul:** On the inside please, in case you were wondering!

**Satpal:** Really? It helps?

**Harsh:** When it comes to medical issues, trust me.

**Gaurav:** Yeah do, but not before getting yourself insured and writing your will!

**Atul:** Harsh, why don't you issue detailed instructions on how to write our wills also, before we leave?

**Kumaril:** Alright, do you think my duffle bag is too small for this trip?

**Gaurav:** Sell it and buy a bigger one. Next question!

**Atul:** Am reading Shackelton. Am on the chapter where the expedition members have not changed their clothes for seven months. Our trip is only for 15 days. I am inspired to manage with two pairs of clothes.

**Gaurav:** No issues. Just carry a hundred room fresheners.

**Satpal:** I have different coloured ribbons that I will issue to each of you. These are meant to be tied to your baggage, to make identifying them easy.

**Gaurav:** So now like little girls with pigtails, we are going to tie ribbons too!

**Supriya:** Do you think I will be able to do the trekking? Should I cancel the trip?

**Gaurav:** Yes. No.

**Supriya**: What's that?

**Gaurav:** Yes, you will be able to. No, you cannot cancel.

**Anita:** Supriya, you are going to fall in love with the place.

**Gaurav:** She has loved only Jolly in her life.

**Anita:** Who is Jolly?

**Gaurav:** A Labrador who is our pet for the last 10 years.

**Supriya:** I can't leave Jolly alone for so many days. He needs lot of care and attention. I am concerned.

**Gaurav:** See, she can live without me for 15 days, but not without Jolly.

**Harsh:** Most people would be happy to live without you for that many days, Gaurav! And Supriya, it's too late to cancel anyway.

**Anita:** Look, all we have to do on the cycling days, is to enjoy the scenery, cheer the cyclists and dive into the snacks. Of course, you will be able to do it! As for the trekking, the place is so beautiful, that it shall egg you on.

**Anurita:** I am not quite a trekking person, but I am really looking forward to this. And Anita and I have decided to write a book on the experience. If for nothing else, just to figure in the book, you must come along!

**Harsh:** I am going there for 'bragging rights'.

**Atul:** I am going for the mountains, the water bodies, the clear skies, the cold, the outdoors, nature, I love them. I could marry the mountains!

**Gaurav:** Anita, you and I are in the same boat. You are nowhere on Atul's list!

**Anita:** It does not matter because Atul knows that eventually the Queen must be kept happy to buy peace in the kingdom!

**Anurita:** Supriya, won't you want to be part of such exciting conversations and alongside finish a trek too?

**Anita:** And if nothing else, a dose of 'Vitamin See' might do you good!

**Supriya:** You guys have your own callings in life. My calling is Jolly. But, fine, I won't cancel.

**Gaurav:** Where is the choice?

Clapping all around.

*While Harsh planned the trip, Anita and Anurita would often sit together to plan this book*

*Photo credit: Sanjeeta Singh*

*Nepal is as plush, as spectacular, as scenic as Tibet*

*Photo credit: Rajiv Popli*

# 6

**_EUDAIMONIA_**

**_You-day-monia_**

*(noun) Origin: Greek*

*The contented happy state we feel when we travel;*

*Happiness from having a good attendant spirit*

## DAY ONE: *To Kathmandu (Nepal)*

That moment had finally arrived. It was Day One of the expedition and the group was leaving for Kathmandu. Eleven of them reached the Ahmedabad airport on Gaurav time, 6.00.27 am! Anurita and Kuldeep reached dot on ABC time, 6.30 am. They were all to fly to Delhi, and then change flight for Kathmandu. Each of them clad in bright red T-shirts could barely contain their excitement as they pranced around eagerly. They conveyed their exhilarated emotions to the airport too, as evidenced by the mixed look of curiosity and bewilderment on many a passenger's face. Soon some were seen checking out the perfume counter, some were drooling over chocolates.

**Satpal:** We are heading for a trek and look at our intention—chocolates, candies and all things fatty!

**Haresh:** We already have enough in our bags, why add more weight?

**Anurita:** The idea is to get on the flight on a sweet note!

**Kuldeep:** You said you are looking forward to losing some extra weight in this trip by taking long, silent walks by the campsites. And chocolates are going to help you with it, are they?

**Anurita:** Chocolates are good when climbing up. They keep you in happy spirits.

**Kuldeep:** Sugar-laced logic indeed!

Rajiv joined them at the Delhi airport. The first thing he did was pick up his T-shirt from Atul and put it on, while the first thing that Harsh did on meeting Rajiv, was to ensure that he pop in a Diamox tablet. They were now in full strength, ecstatic and behaving silly by taking pride in their common attire: red T-shirts and blue jeans. Nothing but their own loud chatter and laughter was punctuating their own loud chatter and laughter over salads and *idlis*!

There may have been women other than Anita and Anurita in my life, and there may have been journeys other than the one that these 14 were about to undertake, but what made it very special for me was the way the two women would exchange detailed notes on the trip several times a day. I loved to eavesdrop on them, and towards the end of the trip felt connected to them. I wonder if they felt it too! Well, to continue, I deduced that the flight to Kathmandu was short—about two hours. At the Kathmandu airport, they received a grand welcome from the tour operators—Explore Himalayas. Clad in uniform green T-shirts, Bharat, Amar and Pandey from this agency, helped them with their bags, and drove them down to Hotel Marshyangdi at Thamel, in two mini buses. It gradually dawned on the group how extensively Harsh had worked on bringing this plan to fruition. Harsh knew the tour operators by name. He was so incredibly hands-on all the time that an unsuspecting observer might be forgiven for assuming that Harsh owned Explore Himalayas. Satpal could not help asking the leader from the tour operator agency:

**Satpal:** What are those heavy files you are referring to all the while?

**Amar:** These are printouts of the email communication we have had with Harsh for arranging this tour.

**Anita:** How many emails would that be?

**Amar:** About 330! This file has almost 500 pages!

**Satpal:** Okay, but why do you need to carry it with you?

**Amar:** We are dependent for our daily arrangements, in fact for the minute-to-minute arrangements for you guys, on these emails. It has so much of detailing, that you know, we plan to use these emails in future to train new recruits for our agency!

**Kumaril:** Alright, if that's the case, what's next on the plan for us in your minute-to-minute plan?

**Amar:** Harsh will now go to our store to check if the bikes and other equipment that we have arranged are in order, and as per request.

They were a bit intimidated but mostly overawed! And repeatedly so!

**Anita:** I hereby rechristen Harsh as HOW—Harsh On Wheels—for his extraordinary energy and eye for detail.

Harsh, Gaurav and Atul left immediately after a late lunch for the store with the representatives of the tour operator. This is where I saw and surmised the three of them for the first time. I immediately realised that we cycles were going to be in the august company of genuine cycle lovers for this expedition. It was rather relieving. I have experienced many a cyclist who rent me, only to jangle my entire body over the roughest of paths for days together, with not a thought spared for my wear and tear. These people were different. Definitely different. We cycles instantly liked them. They checked all of us, the equipment, tents and other camping gear. They also met the boys who were to accompany the expedition to Tibet, and returned to the hotel before sunset, all smiles, completely satisfied with us.

Hotel Marshyangdi, where they were put up, is right in the middle of the market area and has some colourful shops around. How long can you keep away 14 ebullient people from markets! They jaunted into the market that evening, declaring their own intentions of only looking around like innocent window shoppers, as a case of fraudulence. Some of them walked into a shop that was selling down jackets among other things.

**Atul:** What is the weight of the feathers in this jacket?

**Anurita:** Wow, do you have anything in pink?

**Kuldeep:** Do you have warm headgear?

**Anita:** No, I don't like the green one, Atul. Check out the brown one.

**Kumaril:** Hey, they have socks! Can you show me those white ones, please?

**Anand:** Can I take down that raincoat hanging up there?

**Kuldeep:** So many to choose from, this should serve our purpose.

**Anurita**: It's going to be freezing as we go up. I don't like it but I guess these jackets will help. Show me that one!

**Anita**: I think we could pick up most things we want from this one shop.

**Anand:** Do you have a larger size in this?

All spoke simultaneously. The shopkeeper was totally confused and kept looking with wondrous eyes from one to the other, and not a hint of exasperation. He finally communicated to them with the help of a calculator. He would point at something in the shop, quickly type something on the calculator and then energetically thrust it at their faces. Human language sure can take so many forms! This form of communication seemed good enough for the group members as they ended up buying down jackets, trekking sticks, raincoats, ponchos, socks, balaclavas and so on for the trip. Shopping done, on their way back to the hotel, they appreciated all the goodies displayed in the little cafes that dotted the street. Hunger expresses itself in many ways!

For dinner, they visited an Indian friend living in Kathmandu. The friend was warm like English tea as evidenced by the huge and delicious spread on the dining table of his simply furnished residence. The wife was a well-maintained, petite, good-looking woman who seemed to exhibit complete control over the kitchen, the spouse, one pampered kid, and the chit-chat in the drawing room. She, too, was warm in her own meticulous sort of way. The group had the most enlightening conversation with the wife where the decisiveness of her personality was in full force.

**Wife:** You folks are brimming with enthusiasm about this trip. Haven't you gone a little overboard?

**Cyclists:** Have you been there?

**Wife:** No, no way! I am too scared to even think of it!

**Cyclists:** But why are you so sceptical?

**Wife:** I have heard the stay arrangements are pretty filthy.

**Cyclists:** Oh, but we are going to be camping in our own tents till right before reaching Lake Manasarovar, and we will select clean spots.

**Wife:** (Half in bemusement and half patronisingly) I am talking about your trip Manasarovar onward. You know success and failure depend a great deal upon the possession of special information, and I pride myself on that.

**Cyclists:** Well, we have several options—we could let the grime take over our emotions and rule over us, or we could battle it with all the might of our pathological sensibilities. We could even grin and bear it!

**Husband:** Ha ha. All's fair and well in love and war. Love of nature and war with filth!

So long as there was a touch of humour in any situation, as was the parting shot in this case, the group felt reassured. On returning to the hotel, as each one retired to their rooms for a good night's slumber, little were they aware that in the days to come they would literally have only faint memories of cushiony beds, bedrooms, washrooms with running water, food of choice and such blessings that we otherwise take for granted. They were about to embark on the road that leads up to the magical mountain exposing them to a different chapter of life each day that they were there.

# 7

**ALFRESCO**

**Al-fres-co**

*(adv and adj); Origin: Italian*

*Out-of-doors; Fresh;*

*In the open air*

**DAY TWO:** *From Kathmandu to Kodari to Nyalam (China)*

Henceforth, the group became early-risers, though at times to a degree of ludicrousness. At 4.30 am, Kuldeep was one of the earliest to get ready and was walking about with Bharat when one after another, they gathered to a handsome number. By 5.30 am, all were bathed, packed, sandwich-fed and raring to go.

The group was to travel by bus from Kathmandu to Kodari which takes about four hours. It is also the last stop on Nepal side, before the border with China begins. The road to Kodari was so bumpy that the chattering of all their teeth together was good enough to drown the crackling noise of the ageing bus they were seated in, reminding our adventurous bunch of those joyrides that promised dizzying heights at *melas,* which mushroomed across towns and cities during school vacations. The only respite were the *nakas* at regular intervals where the bus was forced to slow down and stop.

We cycles were right behind them in a truck and were bouncing to the tunelessness of the jerky ride amid the sheer beauty and abundance of botanical glory, that is Nepal. River Nyalam was flowing by the side of lush green hills all along the way, often sporting a playful waterfall. The hills were dotted with quite a few quaint looking motels, frequently named Mount View Hotel. One was even named—The Last Resort! I came to know later that three cameras that were undeniably overworked were those of Atul, Kuldeep and Satpal. Sometimes the only way you can preserve memories is on a camera. Yet, the best ones are those made when you keep the camera aside. That is just one among the millions of paradoxes of human life!

The focus of the women on this long trip would meander every other hour or so on what they liked to call 'Loo Tourism'. It is only when you don't have something that you realise the deep and valuable meaning it holds in your life. Due to the absence of large rocks, dense trees/large bushes by the roadside, or even small hillocks with a setting that blocked them from public view on this trip, I am conjecturing that what these women really missed was the 'right place'. The first time they found the 'right place', it was right next to a source of drinking water. What could they do but request the good Lord to forgive them their sins and 'let it go'. The next time they discovered that an umbrella has more uses than one; it can be strategically positioned to safeguard your dignity in a crisis when you are taken hostage by the bladder!

Female porters swarmed them on reaching Kodari, as soon as they alighted from the bus. With their nerves jangled from the ride and persistent negotiations by those porters rattling them even more, they attempted to wear deadpan, bored expressions. None was really in the mood for a good round of bargaining! But these women, they sort of have each other's back, no matter what community, class, country they belong to. The whole act lasted barely five minutes. Soon enough, the women got talking to the porters. And that's when they discovered that Kuldeep spoke fluent Nepali. He was appointed their official translator from thereon.

**Anita:** How much do you earn as a porter?

**Bishnumaya:** About 100 Nepali *rupiyas* a day.

**Supriya**: How much load do you carry at a time?

**Sundari:** Maybe 40 to 45 kg.

**Anita:** Is that your daughter clinging to your legs?

**Chameli:** Yes, I bring her to work.

**Anita:** And Sujata, is that a girl or a boy in the sling across your back?

**Sujata:** A girl. You know, daughters are not liked in our society, so we mothers really have to protect and take good care of them.

**Bishnumaya:** Do you have children?

**Anita:** Yes, I have two grown-up daughters.

**Sundari:** Where is your husband?

**Anita:** (Pointed towards Atul and gave him a smart salute) Police!

All of them understood and laughed. Some things are so universal!

**Chameli:** (speaking to Kuldeep) And how many children do you have?

**Kuldeep:** None yet.

**Chameli**: Where is your better half?

Kuldeep pointed towards Anurita.

**Sujata:** So, when you have children, what would you prefer—a boy or a girl?

**Kuldeep:** I just want one kid, be it a girl or a boy.

**Anurita:** Ah, that's a revelation!

**Supriya:** Sujata, how do you manage to carry the load with a child slung on your back?

Sujata demonstrated how she slid her child from her back to the front and effortlessly carried both—child and load! The Support Group had mixed emotions—wonder, respect, shame, and a feeling of helplessness for the situation of the female porters.

That is when Swati, who had silently slipped away, was seen rushing towards them, excitedly informing that there was a civilised loo right behind the tiny shack they were to lunch in. Our ladies bid their good-byes and moved towards their most-wanted destination.

Post lunch, the group followed a long-drawn and utterly incompetent process to get their passports stamped, for immigration from Nepal into China, by rather friendly and apologetic officials. It was mid-August, hot and balmy; my 14 favourite people on earth were at their wit's end. When they did get their stamped passports back, it was two hours gone! This, however, was nothing compared to what they were about to face at the time of crossing the border.

To cross the border, a bridge that connects Nepal to China, has to be crossed. I was pulled by one of the female porters across the bridge while the group members were following instructions dished out to them on the Nepal side. They were walking aligned strictly behind one another, silently, unsmilingly, heads stable but in consternation, bodies showing no signs of arrogance and eyes never meeting the peering eyes of any one found inside olive green clothes. They were quite a sight—expressionless and comical to onlookers. This, they were told was the only way to prevent attracting unwarranted attention of the gun-toting Chinese military police. The police there watch over you in an unfriendly, rather intimidating manner. Just staring hard does not make them more of policemen than they already were, but these men may not always know this!

The female porters walked effortlessly, carrying the bags on their sturdy backs and pulling us cycles along too. Though some of the group members were only carrying a tiny backpack, I could hear them breathing hard and noisily in this short walk itself. Kodari is at 12,467 feet; perhaps they were feeling the pinch of less oxygen already. On reaching the Chinese side, I gave the word 'incompetence' a new definition, and the group jointly blessed the Nepal officials for the methods they followed in the madness surrounding them.

We cycles were standing by when the group was adequately warned by their Nepal tour operator to be extra nice to the Chinese Customs guys too, and not to get into any argument whatsoever, or they would be simply denied entry. There was pandemonium at Chinese Customs. The group met their Chinese guide, Jamyang, a 25-year-old Tibetan Chinese, just after crossing the bridge. He tried his best to sort things out, but in vain. There were tourists and porters all over the place; each time someone moved they stepped on someone's bags. My group stood in a line, on stairs leading to the Immigration office, which was nothing more than a large rectangular room containing fierce-looking officials in white and blue uniforms. They were out in the sweltering heat for what seemed an eternity.

When their turn came, they were asked to stand in a queue inside the room exactly in the order as mentioned in the visa list, or else... They were then called one by one, stared at, their passport pictures matched hair-to-hair, cell-to-cell, atom-to-atom with their real selves, and then with some indignation, sent forward. Personal belongings of each group member were thoroughly checked, item by item. Next, their entire bodies were scanned, perhaps to check if they had ingested some AK-47s! Sounds funny, I know, but it seemed quite like that.

Since we cycles and camping stuff were accompanying the group, there were a lot of questions that Harsh and Mauley (from the Tour Operators) had to answer. When the group and us cycles, etc. (loosely termed as 'expedition stuff'), finally appeared on the Chinese side, everyone was so relieved, they didn't care a hoot that boxes of bottled mineral water they were carrying were confiscated and several of their personal belongings had magically gone missing too!

Once in China, the first encounter you have is with these fishy-looking characters: young men and women, carrying worn-out sling bags, who come close to the humans, at brushing distance, and whisper right into their ears, 'Dollars for yuan, yuan for dollars'! Jamyang informed that this side of the Immigration office might be the largest city that they would encounter in their entire trip. All members of the group dutifully exchanged their dollars for yuans, with no idea if they had been taken for a ride by something other than a cycle!

From now on the group travelled in the four Land Cruisers, rented by Explore Himalayas from the Chinese side. They had also engaged a huge covered truck to transport their bags, camping equipment, food and other stuff besides us cycles. The idea was to reach Nyalam before nightfall.

Through several cracks in the body of the truck, I could see that the drive to Nyalam, alongside the River Nyalam in spate, was beautiful. The ebullient river gushed across stones of all shapes and sizes, while huge rocks that seemed to have been standing there for centuries, silently watched the goings-on, as if they were representatives of God. Here the waterfalls got even more numerous. They were mostly thin streams falling from a huge height. On the sides of the entire length of the road there was no habitation, but there were houses dotting the hills near the top. The air was clean, cold and carefree.

Each Land Cruiser was permitted to carry only four persons. Anita took the shotgun seat henceforth, to spare the other passengers from witnessing or getting smeared with the yields of car sickness that she was prone to. The driver of her Land Cruiser got chatty with the women in the car.

**Driver:** So, you come from Indeeaaa!

**Anita:** Yes, we are Indeeans!

**Driver:** First time?

**Swati:** Yes. Which part of the country are you from?

**Driver:** Me, Tibetan. You know Tibet.

And he took this as the cue to put on loud Tibetan music.

**Anita:** Yes, we have lot of Tibetans in Indeeaa.

**Driver:** Yes, yes, because of the Dalai Lama.

Silence. The group had been repeatedly warned not to mention the Dalai Lama or even his cat, in China. You could get deported in an instant.

**Driver:** You take care of Dalai Lama. Indeeaa nice!

To the women it seemed like a trap; their eyes instantly met and they refused to give their opinion on the multiple other reasons too why India is nice. Since the driver seemed to be warming towards them, Supriya asked the most vital question that had been beleaguering the women for long.

**Supriya:** Is there any public washroom on the way we could stop at?

**Driver:** Wait. I take you to my friend's *otel.*

**Women among themselves:** (In Hindi) Looks like he is suitably impressed with us!

The friend's '*otel*' had a loo that is better left undescribed!

As the country with the largest population in the world, China indeed ought to be stretched to its capacity, but surprisingly, this part was sparsely populated. You see more uniformed men than local populace. In fact, the route to Manasarovar is marked with men in camouflage and all kinds of other threatening gear, standing guard, at the rate of literally one every 500 metres of the way. They hold their guns in a ready-to-shoot-if-you-so-much-as-look-my-way position. Where they are unable to post live security personnel, they actually put a life-size, all-weather statue of a policeman, with one hand held strangely in 'Hail Hitler' fashion and capable of making Madame Tussaud somersault in her grave!

At intervals of about 15 minutes, right up to Nyalam, they have check points, where the aforementioned young, tall, uniformed, well-built, burly men come and open your car's door without so much as a hint of an apology, for not taking your permission to do so. They demand your passports, claim complete attention, and then one by one the matching of your photographs with you, hair-to-hair, cell-to-cell...begins. Once the intense scrutiny is over, you are permitted to pass through; one feels like having gone through an arduous criminal trial, with the verdict passing in one's favour. Anita, in fact, felt like rushing out of the car at such moments of histrionic importance to celebrate, by looking up emotion-ridden at the sky, and raising hands for thanking the good Lord, Sachin Tendulkar style, sans the bat! Anurita, on the other hand, felt like asking them point blank why they behaved the way they did and why they were the way they were! Notwithstanding the intensity of their feelings, both of course held themselves back.

The only places we did not find these guys dotting the roadsides were in the urban settings. In one such area we got stuck in a traffic jam, because the driver of a huge and brutish container decided to back up into the street suddenly. Being used to traffic jams in India, the women, with sheepish but hasty glances, began scouting the surroundings for possible loo hideouts in preparation for the long wait ahead. Exactly about 15 seconds into the jam, five young men, smartly attired in black uniforms and visor caps, materialised from nowhere in particular. One of them barked some orders to the container driver who immediately and without a whimper went into the side street from where he had appeared. From a distance of at least 300 metres the driver of the container was seen sulking.

Once the road was cleared, the black cats did not disappear into thin air, as one might have expected in the Himalayas; they, instead, lined up in a ready-to-attack-at-the-slightest-provocation stance, narrowed their gaze to slits and peered menacingly at each of our passing vehicles. The group members were not to be daunted this time. It was a laugh riot to watch them adorn severely sombre and helpless looks to allow the Chinese cats their moment of supremacy. As soon as the group had their backs to them, they went back to their gleeful we-are-the-rulers-of-the-world looks. Indeed, how very adaptable humans are!

At 4.30 in the afternoon we reached Nyalam Hotel. It was cold and the jackets and caps were out. We cycles were parked right outside and I could see that the hotel had nice clean rooms. The group had paid extra to get rooms with attached washrooms, a luxury that they would be bereft of for the next

12 days. They were only too willing to make their pockets light for such comfortable causes! However, the first thing Anita did on reaching the room was switch on the television.

**Atul:** What are you doing woman! You do realise that there is no cable here and all programs on TV are in the vernacular?

**Anita:** I know, but I still want to watch.

**Atul:** I should have known. Television is the answer for every frantic prayer of yours to attain infinite bliss!

**Anita:** Hey a Chinese feature film! Not to be missed.

**Atul:** Do you even understand the language? How will you know what's going on?

**Anita:** Who cares about details! Look at the artificial sets, synthetic expressions and cheap glittering clothes. Pretty much like a C-grade Bollywood film. I like this!

**Atul:** I am off for a bath, can't stand this anymore!

**Anita:** How can you be so boring? Go get a life man, even if it's under the shower!

After settling down, they met at 5.30 pm Gaurav time, in the common room of the hotel to be served hot soup prepared by the Tamang brothers (they were the cooks accompanying the group from Explore Himalaya's side). The group was relaxed, covered just enough to take care of the cold outside, sitting on rickety chairs with torn upholstery but comfortable cushions, sipping hot soup, making impolite gurgling noises, and indulging in idle chatter—a great start to a good adventure.

The discussions veered around to Gaurav's favourite topic: time.

**Gaurav:** Impressive! Everyone is here exactly on decided time.

**Atul:** None of us want to be driven to suicide by you over time issues!

**Anita:** By the power vested in me by the government, I hereby christen Gaurav as BOW: Bully On Wheels!

**Supriya:** I think that can be his permanent name.

**Anita:** For that splendidly clever repartee from you, by the power vested in me by nature, cosmos and divinity, I hereby give the name WOW to all the ladies in this group: Wives On Wheels, if you like, but basically, simply WOW!

**Harsh:** Ok, enough of bow, wow, cow, tow! Can we discuss an important issue now? Over to you, Gaurav.

**Gaurav:** We all need to be in sync on this. What time zone are we going to follow—India, Nepal or China?

**Supriya:** Obviously China I would imagine. Why discuss this?

**Gaurav:** If you had waited to speak after I finished you would have known why.

**Supriya:** Ok, why?

**Gaurav:** The Tibetan plateau is not so deep into China, that we can follow China time, and there is no such thing as 'Tibet time'.

**Rajiv:** I checked. Nepal is 20 minutes ahead of India and China is two hours ahead of Nepal.

**Satpal:** You know, both Nepal and Tibet are just above the state of Bihar in India.

**Anita:** Yay! Bihar is my home state. I shall follow Nepal time because it's the friendly neighbour!

**Harsh:** We should all follow Nepal time. Can we please put our watches in sync with Nepal time for the expedition?

**Gaurav:** I will put my watch 20 minutes ahead of Nepal time, because I follow Gaurav time!

**Harsh:** What do you guys plan to do with the rest of the evening?

**Atul:** Go out and explore.

**Harsh:** But I have been told that it is advisable to stay indoors for the first day at least, to acclimatise.

**Atul:** And since when did we start doing what we have been told to do?

**Rajiv:** Look, I cannot stay indoors. Who wants to go out for a walk? Show of hands please.

All hands went up, including Harsh's.

At 6.16.43 pm Gaurav time, they set out for a stroll.

**Rajiv:** What a quiet street!

**Supriya:** (Elated) And so full of dogs!

**Kumaril:** The dogs have such a zombie look about them.

**Anita:** That black one will make a very good lead actor for a horror film.

**Supriya:** Dogs can never be horror material. We humans are.

**Anita:** Hey, why are so many of them suddenly running helter-skelter?

**Satpal:** Ok guys, dog wars have started, just about 100 metres away. Can we move to the other corner, unless you want to take sides?

They moved.

**Kumaril:** Such a strange place. You can't hear a sound except for the barking of dogs. People here either sleep early or prefer to stay indoors.

**Rajiv:** All houses with curtains drawn, no sound; perhaps in reverence to the surrounding mountains.

**Gaurav:** Or in utter veneration to the uniformed personnel strewn everywhere...one can only hazard a guess.

**Supriya:** Hey Anurita and Swati, where were you all this time while we were busy witnessing dog wars?

**Anurita:** Some of these shop owners are quite rude and strange.

**Anita:** Why, what happened?

**Swati:** Anurita and I walked into that corner shop, and asked the lady owner the price of a woollen scarf.

**Anurita:** And you know what she did in response? She slapped her two palms together loudly and rudely yelled *namastey*. Foul mood or strange temperament, we don't know! She sure must've had a bad experience with a tourist before us but that was bizarre.

**Anita:** Oh no, so what did you do?

**Swati:** We simply beat a quick retreat. She made her feelings for us quite clear.

**Gaurav:** It's time anyway.

**Kuldeep:** For what?

**Gaurav:** Dinner!

Just as they were getting back to the hotel, they bumped into a bunch of Gujaratis hailing from Mumbai. With beaming faces, they exchanged warm and friendly smiles and carried on to their rooms. As the group entered the common room of the hotel, they saw Mauley laying dinner on the table. It was noodle soup that day, followed by *dal*, potatoes, rice and *roti*. We were right outside the dining room that day. We heard the slush of the sloppy serving and the continuous clutter of cutlery, once too often. We cycles have never approached food from the angle of eating; it has always been food for thought or for the soul. Watching them eat with utmost pleasure, like little children stealthily munching on chocolates, was delightful, and was cheerfully hailed by the cycle populace by shaking our rear a bit, careful to remain unnoticed. I heard the group talking to Mauley in between his frequent visits to the dining area from the kitchen, sometimes with hot water or tea or more soup and veggies.

**Mauley:** Hope all of you have taken your dose of Diamox tablet for today?

**Harsh:** If anyone has not, please let me know.

They all had.

**Mauley:** You need to drink loads of water on each day that you take a Diamox.

**Anita:** Yeah, at least 50 tons each, or else face sudden kidney failure and sure death.

**Many:** What?

**Anita:** What? Isn't a girl allowed her moment of exaggeration? What has the world come to?

**Harsh:** She is right to an extent. You must drink at least a couple of litres of water per day with Diamox. It is known to cause kidney failure and 'death experience' or sure death if taken over a very long period of time.

**Anita:** And pray how do we define 'long period of time'?

**Harsh:** Relax, it is harmful if taken over several months. For us, about 15 days of Diamox is good enough for taking care of acclimatisation issues.

**Anita:** You mean we shall survive it!

**Mauley:** Of course, you will. We are here to support you.

**Kumaril:** Mauley, how come you have so much energy in this freezing cold?

**Pemba** (cook): Mauley scaled the Mount Everest in 1998. He was all of 24 then, but is very fit even today.

They clapped for Mauley. Respect for him grew by leaps and bounds.

**Mauley:** I plan to climb again next year.

More applause.

**Gaurav:** We also have an Everester amongst us. He climbed when he was 44, much older to you. (Pointing at Atul)

**Mauley:** My salutes to you, Atul Sir!

**Gaurav:** Harsh, why are you so deep in thought?

**Harsh:** For me food time is planning time. We will have to decide on a start time to begin cycling on the day after tomorrow. And for that, we need to check when the first light breaks in the morning. I think I will go out tomorrow at 6 am to take a call.

**Gaurav and Atul:** Count me in too!

# 8

***PULCHRITUDINOUS***

***Pul-krih-tew-di-nuhs***

*(noun) Origin: Latin*

*Physical comeliness; of breathtaking, heartbreaking beauty*

In a life of unceasing joy in the outdoors, acquiring knowledge from the chatter of my riders is a welcome variation. The other cycles consider me strange, because for them the continual bliss of riding is the only stuff that life is made of. My somewhat cerebral nature is just at the edge of their limits of tolerance, and that mercifully, is really the end of the matter for them. Suits me more than fine. Now that I have introduced my friends, allow me to advance your acquaintance to Tibet, a land I admire, to the level of a budding friendship.

When you step into the Tibetan sunshine while gliding on smooth, bituminous roads and look around, you half expect a piece of history to fall into your lap, and show you visions of men in glittering gold and red, running asunder on horseback. I say men, because somehow, the history of the Tibet region of China has scarcely any women in it, except for the queens (of famous kings), whose only recorded contribution is the thrust that Buddhism received, inspired by their activities. The history of Tibet is hardly political. As Sir Charles Bell, a British administrator who travelled widely and lived for almost 19 years in Tibet, put it, 'History, unless it centres on religion, does not appeal to the Tibetan mind'. Stay put, while I put this in perspective.

*One last 'check-up' of cycles in the front yard of Hotel Nyalam, a day before the group began cycling*
*Photo credit: Kuldeep Jadeja*

*Every part of Tibet is picturesque and an ideal campsite*

*Photo credit: Kuldeep Jadeja*

The earliest Tibetans were pastoral, often nomadic; even today many continue to lead the lives of shepherds and yak-herdsmen. It is generally believed that the Tibetans came mostly from East Asia, Assam and Burma. The history of Tibet before the 7th century AD is more folklore than fact. The most well-known epic from ancient history of Tibet is that of Ke-sar, King of the Ling country. Ke-sar, if ever he lived, lived much before Buddhism entered Tibet, when the calendar still showed BC, and a majority of the people were practicing Bon religion. The saga of Ke-sar revolves around his powerful military and its conquests.

The history of Tibet is related with pride and song only after the advent of a teenager king, Songtsen Gampo (he ascended the throne at the age of 13), in the 7th century AD. He is considered to be the greatest king that the Tibetan civilisation saw. Not only a great conqueror, he was also a great administrator. Though Buddhism had taken hold in the country more than 200 years before he came to power, it was the two wives of Songsten, one from China and the other from Nepal, who are credited with its revival and spread. Apparently for want of anything more creative to do, and the deep-set desire to 'feel at home', the queens went about popularising Buddhism. Had the immensity of their work been realised at that time, claims of sainthood for the queens would surely have been heard.

One of the other most significant achievements during Songsten's period was the invention of the alphabet and writing of Tibetan language. He was so enamoured by the Indian manuscripts that he sent his representative all the way to Kashmir in India, to learn writing. The Tibetan writing thus invented was based on the Kashmiri script. Once devised, Songsten could not wait to master it. His unusual solution to the problem of finding time for this pursuit was to shut himself away from royal life for four years; in this period, he learnt both, to read and to write. I think I can safely conclude that his urge to learn, to acquire knowledge, is unmatched in its intensity by any person in his kind of position, till today. Anyway, it was only when there was a threat of mass unrest that he returned to his life as a king. There were two other outstanding kings of Tibet—Tisong Desten and Ralpa Chan. Together, the three are known as The Three Religious Kings, Men of Power.

As far as religion is concerned, it is interesting to note that much before the advent of Buddhism on the scene, the Tibetans were practicing multiple forms of religion, based on beliefs verging on the Shaministic. Mountains and lakes were as precious to them then as they are today. As Sam Van Schaik put it, 'One thing is clear: the Tibetans have always lived in a world swarming with spirits, demons and minor deities. All sorts of names for these still exist in Tibet. Sometimes it is said that the world is ruled by three types of spirit: the *Lha* in the heavens, the *Nyen* in the air and on the peaks of mountains, and the *Lu* in the underworld and rivers. The mountain deities were particularly revered, with each clan having its own mountain and the clan leaders considering themselves the descendants of the mountain's divine embodiment.' These beliefs are sometimes loosely categorised as Bon religion.

An important phase in the history of Tibet was the rule of the priest-kings. By the 14th century, Buddhism had once again weakened its hold on the region mainly owing to unsystematic practice, but reform was on the anvil. The priesthood existing at that time comprised of the Red Hats, among others. Tsong Kapa or The Man from the Land of Onions, born in 1358, initiated reforms. He instituted a stricter code of morals, celibacy and teetotalism for his disciples, who came to be known as the Yellow Hats. Tsong Kapa's successor was Ganden Truppa, who continued the good work. After Truppa, an infant who was born two years after his death, was appointed in his place, as it was believed that Truppa's spirit had passed on to the child. This identification of a reincarnate became the established system thenceforth for selecting the next incumbent.

The fourth in the series of reincarnations, Sonam Gyatso is highly revered. He is credited to have spread Buddhism not only in Tibet but also in Mongolia. It was he who received the title of Dalai Lama Vajradhara from Altan Khan, the Mongolian chieftain. The literal translation of the title is, 'The all-embracing Lama; The Holder of the Thunderbolt'. Sonam Gyatso accepted the title as the Fourth Dalai Lama, naming the previous three also as Dalai Lamas. Thus the tradition that began in the 16th century AD, continues to this day. The Dalai Lamas are the Priest Kings in whom many Tibetans believe and follow even today. With the merging of Tibet into China, this tradition has taken a different turn on which I am not knowledgeable enough to comment.

Coming back to the tradition of identifying the new Dalai Lama based on the 'passing of the spirit', it is interesting to note how the present and Fourteenth Dalai Lama interprets 'reincarnation'. Thomas Laird, through a series of conversations, questioned the Dalai Lama on this issue. The following conversation is quoted from his book, *The Story of Tibet, Conversations with the Dalai Lama*:

> 'If someone asks me whether I am the reincarnation of the Dalai Lama,' he said, 'then I answer, without hesitation, yes. This does not mean I am the same being as the previous Dalai Lama. Some Dalai Lamas are a manifestation of Manjushri. Some are a manifestation of Chenrizi. Chenrizi is the manifestation of compassion. Manjushri is the manifestation of wisdom. I have a special connection with the Thirteenth Dalai Lama and

the Fifth Dalai Lama. I feel I can say I have some kind of connection with the previous Dalai Lamas, some of the previous masters, with Chenrizi, even with the Buddha. This English word connection you keep using, it doesn't give a true explanation of everything that you mean when you use it. It has a number of meanings. It can mean that there was a personal connection; we might have been born in the same time during a past life; a teacher and student; or a ruler and a subject or we might even have been spiritual friends. There could have been a personal life connection. Also, there can be other factors...'

This 'connection' in some lifetime or in some universe, with this place, I believe, is what pulled the 14 members of this expedition to Tibet, and made them fall in love with it.

In the complex history of Tibet, it would be amiss of me, if I forget to mention Milarepa, considered to be the greatest Tibetan yogi who lived in the 10th century AD. He was the disciple of Marpa, popularly known as The Great Translator for his humongous contribution to Tibetan culture, in translating several works (chiefly related to tantric yoga) of Indian origin into Tibetan. Marpa made several trips to India just to collect manuscripts, which he would later translate himself. Milarepa is known to have lived a life of crime, before he went the righteous way, somewhat like the Indian saint Valmiki. Milarepa's teachings are so universal, it is believed that no religion can rightly claim him as its exclusive preserve. Truth-seekers all over the world study Milarepa even today.

Milarepa learnt the Indian form of verse called the *doha*, from his Guru Marpa's many collections of Indian manuscripts, and merged it with the typical dramatic form of Tibetan verse. As Sam Van Schaik put it, 'Whereas in the imperial period,

> 'In Milarepa's view, none of the world's methods of intellectual development are essential to the attainment of Wisdom; Right Knowledge was, for him, not to be won by study of books, nor by making professions of faith. Many of the most learned and cultured saints of Tibet and India have been illiterate. Of these things Milarepa bore witness as follows:
>
> *"Accustomed long to meditating on the Whispered Chosen Truths,*
>
> *I have forgot all that is said in written and in printed books.*
>
> *Accustomed long to application of each new experience to mine own growth spiritual,*
>
> *I have forgot all creeds and dogmas.*
>
> *Accustomed long to know the meaning of the Wordless,*
>
> *I have forgot the way to trace the roots of verbs, and source of words and phrases."'*
>
> Source: W Y Evans Wentz

Tibetan poetry had celebrated military victories, Milarepa's songs celebrated his victories over self-clinging and the negative states of mind that it engenders. Though, viewed from the outside, Milarepa's life as a hermit was terribly spartan, his inner experiences are joyously related in the many songs attributed to him:

*This is a delightful place of hills and forests.*
*In the mountain meadows the flowers bloom.*
*In the woods dance the swaying trees.*
*For monkeys it is a playground.*
*Birds sing tunefully,*
*Bees fly and buzz.*
*From day till night rainbows come and go,*
*In summer and winter the sweet rain falls,*
*In spring and autumn the mist and fog rolls.*
*In solitude in this pleasant place*
*I, Milarepa, happily stay,*
*Meditating on the empty and luminous mind.'*

Milarepa's verse above relates to the joy that lies deep within each of us, even within cycles, in that undisturbed, unruffled, calm realm, that we call the soul. But it is quoted here because it also aptly and monumentally represents for a traveller, the essence that is Tibet. Tibet is spell-bindingly packed with the gifts of nature, but sometimes when for miles you stare into bare plains, brilliantly empty of habitation as well, the curiously disproportionate distribution of bounties does not bother you; it is rather hypnotic. In fact, the best thing about this entire trip was that the cycles and cyclists were always completely in 'touch' with the mesmerising outdoors. There were no visits to museums to gaze admiringly at strange artefacts and make intelligent comments thereafter; no architectural wonders to be visited that are so ravaged by time that one is almost terrified to step into them; no subjecting of the cyclist's Eustachian tubes and my aesthetic sensibilities to the rote-learnt and dramatised versions of history from tour guides at touristy places. Wow, this was different! It would be hot, windy, cold, and rainy—all at once, but for us, every bit of it was one splendid adventure.

Geographically speaking, Tibet as a region can be divided into three natural divisions: one, the Northern Plains consisting of several plains and valleys, all at the minimum elevation of 16,000 feet; two, the valleys of the Indus, Sutlej, Tsang-po and Brahmaputra rivers (all rising near Lake Manasarovar) in the West and South; and three, the mountains and valleys of Eastern Tibet. The Indus and Sutlej rivers rise from the slopes of Mount Kailash. We were in the South-West area of Tibet. Tibet is known as the Roof of the World, because with an average elevation of 16,000 feet, it is indeed the highest region on earth. Tibet is home to several high-altitude lakes, including

Manasarovar, and some of the tallest mountains of the world, including the tallest, Everest. The south side of Everest falls in Nepal, and the north side is in Tibet. Mount Kailash, where the group was headed (its Tibetan name is Khang Rinpoche), and several other mountains sacred to the Buddhists, are located all across Tibet.

The people are simple at heart, cheerfully industrious, amenable to foreigners and lead a life full of challenges. The women are beautiful, and especially look divine with the several pieces of jewellery that they wear like epaulets. The young men are, more often than not, given to tallness and ruggedness in particular, and handsomeness in general—a lethal combination! Children exhibit the reddest of cheeks and the most beatific of smiles. They are so gentle and endearing that you may struggle to really stop yourself from snatching a kid or two from their parents for your own delight.

The houses in the villages are very few, but typical. There is a stone base in sturdier houses, which is given a miss sometimes for economic reasons. Above the base is the walling that comprises of mud bricks; these are cemented together with cow dung and straw. These days, bricks and cement are increasingly used. There is one door and very few windows, in the interest of protection from the harsh winters, snow, dust storms, etc. The ceiling made of wood is supported by pillars. The house is typically painted grey on the outside, with windows and doors decorated in maroon, yellow and blue colours while furnishings are simple. I came across several earthenware pots, copper vessels, ladles and large spoons and bowls in the tiny residence-cum-motels I managed to peep into while being parked outside. Water being a scarce commodity, all the empty vessels in the house are used to store it.

A sense of what life has been over the past decades and centuries can be gauged from the fact that the primary occupation a majority of Tibetans still engage in is raising livestock (sheep, cattle, yaks, horses). Tibetans are a proud community and despite certain politico-regional issues, they like to assert themselves, even if in anonymity.

***I AM A TIBETAN***

*I'm a Tibetan*
*My skin is the colour of ancient bronze, but*
*My favourite colour is dark red*
*I'm a Tibetan*
*The teachings of my ancestors are engraved on my bones*
*The sound of horses' hooves flows in my veins*
*Fragrant barley ale fills up both my eyes*
*Enchanting gesar flowers bloom on my body*
*I'm a Tibetan*
*Tibetan: a name which is matched by reality*
*Tibetan: standing on the earth, touching the heavens*
*Remember don't ask me for my surname*
*My surname is not Li, my surname is not Wang*
*If you insist on asking for my surname*
*I'll tell you I am a follower of the Buddha*
*I am a strong nation blessed by the Tibetan Gods*
*My left shoulder is a hawk*
*My right shoulder is a yak*
*My body is a lamp under the statue of the Buddha,*
*Never extinguished.*

***Anonymous***

Source: Sam van Schaik

The group learnt about the staple diet of Tibetans from their drivers. All through the expedition, the drivers ate/drank either of the following three foods: *tsampa,* a dough made from barley flour; dried yak cheese; butter tea. Some of the ladies and Satpal tried sampling *tsampa*, but had to give up trying on first bite. The *tsampa* is almost bland or perhaps the Indian spiced-up palettes are unable to appreciate the simplicity of basic and original flavours. The yak cheese has a certain smell to it, which makes it difficult getting used to, I guess. Their tea is made of good clean cholesterol, also known as butter in human parlance; it is a heart attack waiting to happen, unless you measure up to the fitness standards of Superman or of a Tibetan!

During the entire expedition, wherever we passed in Tibet, we did not see any systematic dwellings. In the almost 550 km stretch that we covered by road to reach Lake Manasarovar, the number of habitations, Tibetans, and vehicles we saw, were less than the spokes in my single wheel. Most houses stood in glorious seclusion beside the roads. For miles together there would be the emptiness of space and the cosmos: no shops, no gas stations, nothing. The group would often wonder how locals got their water, daily requirements, and electricity. And what about a primary school for children? We never saw a single hospital, school, government office of any kind (except for the tiny check posts), markets (except for one isolated shop selling foreign chocolates and bakery stuff), car repair services, or even a congregation of people, say for a wedding ceremony, along the way. Even the total number of cycles we saw other than us 11, were in single digit. This kind of expansive and arresting nothingness sounds eerie, and is perhaps the reason for the extreme hardships faced by the locals, but none in the group was complaining, for none had ever seen a place as respectably eminent, as precious and charming as this.

The outdoors in Tibet are not without their share of apprehensions for travellers, for it is a country where the dogs are so large and strong that they are capable of killing a tiger.

King cobras, the world's largest venomous snakes, could be one of the sleeping partners in your tents; wild dogs and wild cats are aplenty—you could see more of them than Tibetans at places; Himalayan snow bears and snow leopards could be spotted looking lip-smackingly down from the upper reaches at their potential prey, that is you. But somehow, and quite inexplicably, once you venture into this part of the world, these matters become trifling before the vastly and multitudinously endowed surroundings and imposing silence. Here silence speaks, and we cycles love to noiselessly merge with the silence!

What unceasingly amazed me were the well-tarred, four-lane roads all through (except for a patch near Saga). We could ride so smoothly, that if our cyclists wished, they could easily have lapsed into practicing riding meditation. Some of them probably did, perhaps unknowingly. The Support Group members would ride in the Land Cruisers in Tibet. They would either absorb the place in complete silence or let out *oohs* and *aahs* at recurrent intervals at the multiple, memorable views along the way. However, their driver, as you shall see, would insist on making futile attempts to break their concentration and conversation, by playing a CD of Tibetan disco songs, with a certain repetitive rapture. After every few attacks of this nature on their auditory nerves, the ladies convinced of the need to recognise the impasse between the driver and them, would take a shot at thawing it, by conversing with the driver.

**Anita:** How long have you been driving tourists around here?

**Driver:** Twenty years.

**Supriya:** How many times have you done this trip?

**Driver:** Many 'tie'. (Sometimes the Tibetans do not say the first or the last syllable; here 'time' becomes 'tie'.)

**Anita:** What if this vehicle breaks down?

**Driver:** Then stay 'ere' till we fix it.

**Anurita:** And do you know how to fix it?

**Driver:** No.

End of conversation. Back to loud Tibetan disco music!

# 9

*UKIYO-E*

***Ooki-o-eh***

*(noun) Origin: Japanese*

*Literally 'the floating world';*

*Used to represent an attitude of living in the moment, detached from the bothers of life*

**DAY THREE:** *At Nyalam*

Anita woke up with a frightful start as she saw someone creeping into her room in the dead of night. Whenever fear gets the better of her, she simply freezes without a sound; her limbs become almost lifeless; thoughts of paranormal activity cling to her like lycra shorts on a cyclist, and her face is a study in psychosomatic disorders!

'It's all right. Go back to sleep.'

That was Atul. Relief flooded her being, but the experience had left her a little peevish.

**Anita:** Why? When? How? What's going on?

**Atul:** We had gone out to check the morning light. But imagine, it is 6 am and pitch dark outside!

Anita has a brain abidingly fascinated with rest, and wired for large doses of sleep. Though she does not have Gaurav-like time-keeper-to-the-nation expertise, she can tell the time at any point of the night by simply counting the number of yawns she gets while attempting to speak a full sentence.

**Anita:** (Yawning) Please check my watch; it's lying on the table there. It may not be more than 4 am. Who told you it is 6 am?

**Atul:** Oh no! You are right. It is 3:54:53 Gaurav time. I think Harsh and Gaurav forgot to sync their watches to the new time zone, and I too just went along with them on their first knock.

**Anita:** I thought it was just in the waking hours. But Gaurav and his OCD for time seem to be terrorising you even in your sleep now!

Allow me a little contemplation here on the phenomena of sleeping, dreaming and being awake. As a cycle, I know no sensations unless they are transmitted by humans, and for me the world stands still as I neither sleep nor dream. The states of sleeping and waking in humans are magical. The dream objects/matter can be very different from the waking objects/matter. Just as the dream objects disappear completely on waking up, the emotions, sensations, thoughts, experiences of waking up disappear in dream state. Which one is true? Is every experience, every sensation, both true and untrue? How very queer, yet interesting it is, that nothing is stable. I am convinced that the external world is maintained by the thoughts of humans. Is it possible that the entire universe, including us cycles, is nothing but a creation of human thoughts?

On that rare note, let us get back to the story. So, Atul went right back to Harsh's room to inform him of the folly. They resolved to check again at local time 5.30 am. The taking of such a vital decision prompted Harsh, Gaurav and Atul to catch up on their remaining sleep, snoring and all; not a second was wasted. They got up once again at Nepal time 5.30 am, ventured out in the deliciously cold streets of Nyalam, and determined that 6.30 am would be the time for the start of the cycling expedition the following day.

Kuldeep got up early and was ready by 7 am. He took a walk outside and headed towards the kitchen where the cooks were busy preparing breakfast. He gently asked about their welfare. The cooks were not used to this. Most groups they had worked for, had not bothered to even know if they were ever christened by their parents or whether they preferred to be in a state of nameless stupor. You can well imagine how welcome Kuldeep was amongst them. By 9 am, everyone else was up and nourished by a sumptuous breakfast.

We cycles were taken out in the sunny courtyard of the hotel to be prepared for the next day for riding the roads of Tibet. The three brothers accompanying us—Mauley Tamang (the Everester), Make Tamang (our head cook) and Pemba Tamang (the assistant)—were of great assistance. It always feels good to be groomed. And mind you, overhauling us cycles is a form of physical exercise, too, quite like riding. The only difference is that overhauling being a stationery exercise, you don't feel the wind hit you with the force of an unshaken belief!

**Harsh:** Please choose a cycle and try it out. Once you have chosen it, adjust it according to your requirements. Remember, we want no mechanical surprises. And don't forget to stick your name label on your chosen cycle.

**Gaurav:** I need to put the cleats on.

**Harsh:** You can take my tool box.

**Satpal:** Does anyone have a cycle pump? No? No problem. I will make one right now out of some small hardware that should be available in the market.

**Anita:** Where did you learn to do these odd jobs, Satpal?

**Satpal:** In my head, I think. I like doing it.

**Kumaril:** What are the ladies up to while we work?

**Anita:** We like to keep a watch over men at work. No, actually, we just like to watch men. Period. But seriously, we are just sunning ourselves.

**Supriya:** And drying shampooed hair. Last shampoo for the next 10-odd days.

**Anita:** Hey Mauley! Is that your cycle? Are you cycling too?

**Mauley:** Yes, Madam, I am. What about you?

**Anita:** I will, in my next birth. In this one, I have yet to learn cycling. And you Jamyang, aren't you cycling?

**Jamyang:** No. Get 'tarrit'. And then much 'tenzin'.

**Anita:** Wow! What was that?

**Kuldeep:** Get 'tired'. And then much 'tension'. Ha ha....

**Anurita:** Hey, there is pin-drop silence at this place. Our chatter is the only sound. Let's go take a walk on the main street outside the hotel.

**Supriya:** Anita, Swati and I had gone out earlier. Apart from us there was not a soul on the street outside.

**Anita:** And Swati in her pink trousers and pink jacket was a picture in pink! But I found something very strange.

**Anurita:** What?

**Anita:** The entrance door of almost every house on the street is ajar and you can see women sitting and picking lice from their children's heads. Hygiene seems to be an issue on this street.

**Rajiv:** It must not be hygiene, but the lack of clean water and sanitation facilities.

**Anurita:** At least you saw humans other than shopkeepers. I think I'd like to set out for a walk, some gazing and window shopping.

**Anita and Supriya:** Again!

**Anurita:** Oh yes! I love doing that—watching display windows, some art popping out, expressions on faces behind, even exchanging occasional smiles and pleasantries. If I don't set out, I'd feel so incomplete!

**Atul:** I am joining you purely in the interest of providing high-level protection. Cop duty calls!

**Anurita:** Ah! Such selflessness!

**Anita:** Nothing, not even selflessness can come between me and window-shopping! I am in the definitely-going-back-there list. Let's go, Anurita!

**Rajiv, Swati, Kumaril, Kuldeep, Supriya, Gaurav...:** Me too!

Post dinner, the world slowed down for the group. Now that their basic needs were taken care of, life seemed to be offering several free moments to take vital pending decisions. Anita decided to wash her hair for posterity's sake and Supriya decided to go out and take one last longing look at the zombie dogs. The rest of the group was trying hard to stare into the vacant sky, probably to get into the groove of electricity-less days ahead. At about 8 pm, almost suddenly, Haresh, Satpal, Supriya, Swati, Gaurav, Anita, Atul, Kuldeep and Anurita set out towards the market for a walk in the hushed locale, careful not to laugh too loud on the silly jokes of Atul and Gaurav. They walked right up to Nyalam river. It was cold there, about 5 degrees Celsius, and the wind was broadcasting its sharp presence by cutting through the layers of clothes. Meanwhile, Harsh was still busy making crucial assessments. As soon as the group returned to the hotel, Harsh announced that he would take lead for all of the estimated 55 km of the first day of cycling and the rest of the cyclists could draft right behind.

*Drafting is the system in which one cyclist takes the lead, and the others tuck close behind the lead in a line, to reduce wind resistance for them and thereby spend less energy. Due to vast stretches of empty spaces in Tibet, the wind has a free-for-all attitude. Wind resistance is a mild word for Tibet. It should be wind might in full throttle!*

It wasn't as though Harsh was exercising the full force of his personality here, he is made like that. He would rather do the most challenging task himself, so that others could strengthen their chances of ending up with 'bragging rights' too!

But truth be told, it is tough for the person who takes the lead, and Tibet was not about to be gentle on the cyclists!

# 10

***MISDEEM***

***Miss-deem***

*(verb) Origin: English*

*Misjudge; to have a wrong opinion of; (to misdeem one's ability, for example)*

**DAY FOUR:** *Nyalam to Peiku Tso via Nyalam Pass*

Most of the group members had spent ridiculous amounts of time collecting knick-knacks for this tour, shopping for that exact coffee mug and spoon or wonder wipes or some such thing and packing them precisely *a la* Harsh, in bags which appeared like sumo wrestlers when only half full. Even if one thing was out of place, they would try to repack in the exact manner as it was earlier. It was a drill in extraordinary patience, meticulousness and discipline. But for them the attraction of that one final hot water bath at Nyalam, in a closed-door bathroom, where your dignity was not at risk, was well worth all the trouble of unpacking and repacking.

Hence, to be able to bathe, repack and report at 5.30 am ABC time, they were up at 4 am the next day. They once again opened their bags, dissected them, and ended up with clothes and belongings strewn all over the place giving it the tsunami-hit look that is the hallmark of a teenager's room. Finally, they simply, quickly and messily, repacked. The initial enthusiasm to emulate Harsh's perfectionism was already fading. Of course, in his own case, even in moments of weakness, Harsh did not let go of his method or discipline in packing. Harsh is

*Amidst cheering by the Support Group, cycling begins from Nyalam*
*Photo credit: Atul Karwal*

*Negotiating Nyalam Pass*
*Photo credit: Atul Karwal*

all about gravitas in dealing with life! See below his written directions to the tour operators and be convinced:

**Level of Services: 'Harshisms'!**

**Vehicle Movements**:

a. The staff will remain with the truck to dismantle tents, etc. after the convoy leaves.
b. Staff will load the luggage with the tents, etc. in the truck and leave for the next destination.
c. Staff will reach the next destination ahead of the convoy and set up tents, etc.
d. One Land Cruiser will stay close to riders in the front while progressing slowly and keeping them in eye contact all the time.
e. One Land Cruiser will stay behind the last rider—keeping him/her in eye contact all the time and never overtake the last rider.
f. Under no circumstances the last Land Cruiser will lose sight of the last rider at any point.
g. Two Land Cruisers will stay in the middle (between the first and the last riders.)
h. About 10 km before the destination, the first Land Cruiser will go ahead and remain parked on the road side to indicate the camp site.
i. The drivers of the Land Cruisers must be informed in advance about slow movement and frequent stops by Explore Himalaya.

(Note: These will be primarily decided in consultation with the bicycle riders the previous evening. A meeting with Explore Himalaya staff, drivers and riders at the time of dinner will decide the next day's plans.)

At 5.30 am when they began to trickle into the dining room, they found Gaurav and Supriya already there and through with breakfast. Gaurav time was petrifying! When the cyclists got ready to move, the Support Group cheered them up and began moving in front of them in the Land Cruisers.

The idea was that the Support Group would always move ahead of the cyclists and wait every 4–5 km to make available water, energy drinks and eatables to them, and generally ensure that all was well. The first wait at about half kilometre was over two hours long. Apparently, at the first pedal, the chain on Haresh's cycle broke. By the time they were ready to move again it was 8 am. To add to the muddle, they experienced a headwind right away.

**The wind can take sides**

A tailwind blows in the direction of travel. It increases your speed and reduces time to reach the destination. You can give in to the wind, literally, and allow it to control your direction.

A headwind blows right into your face and opposes your movement forward. It is a cause of concern and frustration to cyclists.

A tailwind is loved to the point of a relationship in the offing. A headwind is the object of obstruction and dismay.

**Anurita:** No matter how well we plan and how meticulous we are, hiccups remind you about the imperfection that is life.

**Swati:** This journey is like a guru for us.

**Anurita:** Indeed, there's nothing that helps you know more about life and human nature better than travel. Shall I read out some interesting one-liners on travel from this little pocket book I picked up?

**Swati:** Why not? Time or the lack of it does not seem to be the issue in Tibet!

**Anurita:** Then here you are:

- The world is a book and those who do not travel end up reading only a page.
- We must take adventures in order to know where we truly belong.
- Travel makes one modest for you realise what a tiny space you occupy in the world.
- Nothing develops intelligence like travel.

**Anita:** Yeah, I vouch for that one. I can already feel my grey matter multiplying in geometric progression! World, you may await my domination! Give me more!

**Anurita:** Coming your way, me lord!

- Travel is the only thing you buy that makes you richer.
- It's not the journey or the destination; it's who you are travelling with.
- I'd rather have a passport full of stamps than a house full of stuff.
- Travel while you are fit and able. Don't worry about the money, just make it work for experience is far more valuable than money ever will be.
- It is better to travel well than to arrive.

  And now for my personal favourite:

- If something good happens, travel to celebrate. If something bad happens, travel to forget it. If nothing happens, travel so that something happens.

**Swati:** Travel commandments! I love them.

**Anurita:** It's wonderful to be with the like-minded.

The cyclists had formed three groups. One that took the lead consisted of Harsh, Gaurav, Atul and Haresh. The next lot had Kumaril and Anand, and the last one had Satpal, Rajiv and Sanjeeta. They were cycling now, on the roads, negotiating the sharp turns, breathing in the scenery, delighted in their childlike enthusiasm. When they would bend down on our handlebars, we could feel their hearts pounding away with the rhythm; that was further impetus for us to bound over the roads like a thing of life. Trees, bushes, hills, clouds would pass us, and we would pass them. From the moment we started, we became part of a mellifluous symphony.

The Support Group also split into two vehicles—Swati, Supriya and Anita in one and Anurita and Kuldeep in another. It wasn't too long before Anurita caught the girls in the other car hungrily attacking the snacks earmarked for cyclists, when she realised she was missing out on much more than her share of girl talk. She soon hopped in with them. Kuldeep was thenceforth left in 'solitary' confinement with a 'tenzin'-prone Jamyang and the boys from Nepal, who preferred to catch up on sleep in preparation for the hard work at the campsites.

Along the way, they stopped by often, for photographs. The picturesque landscape simply had to be captured for recalls and retellings in the future. In fact, the entire lot was photo-active—the cyclists and the Support Group, both. They also passed by some traditional homes that seemed to pop up out of nowhere. There were kids playing by the road, their mothers oblivious of vehicles passing and stopping by. The children waved energetically to everyone who noticed them. It wasn't just a wave though, they even pointed towards the fruits in the car and asked for them. On receiving them, the victorious smiles on their faces seemed to indicate that they had won some war! And exactly in post-war fashion, they would prance around with the fruit held aloft like a trophy won. At one point, gripped by curiosity, Sanjeeta decided to stop cycling and explore one of the bylanes alongside the main road, dotted with a few small, two-room houses. Led by her, a few went in to see one of those houses, climbed what looked like a ladder outside, and posed for pictures with the Tibetan family.

Meanwhile, watching the cyclists toil uphill, the Support Group members felt the need to assert their sense of adventure too.

**Anita:** The high point of adventure in my life has been giving birth to two kids. Nothing can compare to that.

**Swati and Supriya:** Me too!

**Anurita:** I have yet to arrive to that stage. But I can imagine what it must feel like, having watched parents indulge us. I think raising children too must be one of the best adventures life offers. I also look at it this way… raising a child is like a test you take, the result of which shows up a good 15–20 years hence!

**Anita:** Nothing compares to times spent with children.

**Supriya:** You know, while the men are cycling for adventure, we are having our own little adventure looking for private places in the flat surroundings for a loo break!

Some giggling and loo talk followed, but soon they got back to talking about life, nature and beyond.

As soon as you get out of Nyalam, the landscape becomes an artist's delight. In Tibet, God does not draw boundaries where the sky begins or where the rolling hills end. It all appears like one serene piece of nature, knit like a fabric in the vibrant colours of Mother Earth that is so soft to touch and feel, you wouldn't want to let go. The numerous shades of the hills or

> 'In a car you're always in a compartment, and because you're used to it you don't realize that through that car window everything you see is just more TV. You're a passive observer and it is all moving by you boringly in a frame.
>
> On a cycle the frame is gone. You're completely in contact with it all. You're IN the scene, not just watching it anymore, and the sense of presence is overwhelming.'
>
> – Robert M Pirsig, *Zen and the Art of Motorcycle Maintenance*

the sky that keep changing every few kilometres already look like paintings created by different artists.

Unbelievable and amazing are the ways of God, for who else could plan such a big world with diverse people, cultures, food and lifestyle on one large canvas of nature.

After about 15 minutes of cycling from Nyalam on gentle slopes, the cyclists encountered a sharp uphill slope that carried on for miles together. In the first half hour itself there was a height gain of almost 500 metres. In fact, it turned out that the Google-map-based estimation of the distance and elevation was incorrect. The first 60 km were all uphill, and steeply so. Neither the cyclists nor the cycles had bargained for this.

There is this romantic, wild and uninhibited view we hold on to with regard to adventure; we gloat in it for a while, until the body gives up with a thud! After the first 15 minutes or so of romance with the beautiful Tibetan countryside, the headwind and the clear roads, all ideas of a dreamy life took a backseat as it got difficult for the cyclists to breathe. Performance and intention ran into conflict with each other. It was clear that anyone who was willing or even attempting to ride their cycles uphill towards the Nyalam Pass, was not a glutton for just any punishment; they were, in fact, demanding torture!

The cyclists' adventure had truly begun, as you might deduce from the milestones of the first day of cycling:

- After about 5 km, Sanjeeta was the first casualty. Her body had given up and she could no longer take the tough climb. She put her cycle back in the truck and sat down in one of the Land Cruisers for the rest of the journey that day. Wise decision, as we shall see later!
- The cyclists had wrongly estimated 55 km; it was, in fact, 90 km of cycling that day, of which 60 km were steep

uphill, leading to Nyalam Pass. The elevation was rising up from 12,500 feet to 17,500 feet!

- By the end of 20 km, the rest of the eight cyclists were dog tired.
- Around 25 km later, Kumaril developed high fever and had to be rescued.
- Just about 30 km were covered when Anand, Haresh and Rajiv could take it no more. They boarded the Land Cruisers.
- The sloggers that remained were Harsh, Gaurav, Atul and Satpal.

We four cycles had to strain very hard to ply. The cyclists put more weight on the cycle in a steep uphill climb and their exhaustion and breathlessness get conveyed to us. When only about 5 km were left for the four cyclists to reach Nyalam Pass perched at 17,500 feet, the rest of the group decided to drive up to the Pass and wait there. Bad decision, as they eventually realised.

**Supriya:** The wind here is so sharp and cold. It is rendering all the layers of warm clothing on me thoroughly useless.

**Rajiv:** It is a Pass after all. The wind passes through strongly here, in fact, excessively and unpardonably so!

**Supriya:** Perhaps you guys are hungry. Shall I take the sandwiches out?

**Anurita:** There speaks a mom, but I can't eat since I am feeling uncomfortable. You need not wait for me, Supriya. You go ahead.

**Supriya:** Oh, I gave away my packed lunch to the stray dogs we found on the way.

**Swati:** Why is Kuldeep looking so dishevelled?

**Anurita:** We both have a terrible headache, though not sure why! We haven't quite exerted ourselves.

**Rajiv:** It's the height. We have climbed 5,000 feet in five hours. The process of acclimatisation requires that you climb not more than 1,000 feet a day. And in case you do, you don't stay at that height too long if you get any signs of hypoxia such as headache, breathlessness and nausea. But here we are, awaiting the cyclists.

**Anita:** That must be the reason for the way I feel. Alright people, now that I get it, I need an undisturbed 10 minutes.

**Anurita:** What for?

**Anita:** I am about to throw up and would prefer to do it gracefully!

**Anurita:** Come, I will be with you.

**Anita:** Yes please, moral support is a prerequisite for this outrageous act!

**Haresh:** We must start going down the Pass now. If we don't lose height soon we will have to deal with large-scale, sudden sickness. Sanjeeta is not too well. Kumaril's fever is shooting up and he is finding it tough to breathe. Kuldeep is totally out of gear. And look at what Anita is up to.

**Rajiv:** But we must wait for the cyclists. If we are finding it so difficult, imagine their condition.

**Supriya:** Oh yes, we must wait.

Meanwhile, Kuldeep and a highly febrile Kumaril came and joined them.

**Kumaril:** There is some animated discussion going on amongst the five Tibetan drivers. By the tone of it, I can figure they are hatching a plan.

**Kuldeep:** We wouldn't know unless they communicate to us in a language we understand, but the little bits and pieces I could catch from what resembled Nepali, it has something to do with money.

**Supriya:** Could they be in high 'spirits'? You know what I mean?

**Kumaril:** The fever may have affected my sense of smell, but not my judgment. They all appear sober to me.

**Kuldeep:** No, they don't dare to drink and drive here. This is China, it is a strict country.

**Sanjeeta:** Well, ours is to wait—wait for the cyclists and wait for the drivers to tell us what's on their mind.

They waited for more than an hour on the Pass. At only 50 percent of the oxygen available at this height as compared to sea level, each passing minute was difficult to take.

Thirty-nine-year-old Mauley thought it was a good time for some 'encouraging' talk and began telling those within his hearing distance about how he climbed Mount Everest when he was just 24, in all of 23 hours! He then got talking about Mount Kailash since that is where this group was headed for, and from past experience, he knew that the mountain would generate enough energy to divert the group's attention from the immediacy of losing height.

**Mauley:** This is the 37th time I would be going to Mount Kailash. As for *parikrama,* I have done it 13 times. Each time is similar in a way, and yet offers a different perspective. The experiences vary depending on the people/group we have along. I recall there was once a group of 140 people. Though they were all very tough physically, but managing and handling the intra-group dynamics was one big task!

**Kuldeep:** Do you stay in touch with all the different people you come across each time, or do they stay in touch?

**Mauley:** Oh yes, people come and go. No one stays in touch with us. We are accompaniments in their trip, which some term as mission, but that's about it. Lots of thoughts and opinions are expressed by them too, but once they go, that's the end of it all. But, you know, nature is fun. It keeps me happy. There are times I feel like quitting this job and pursuing a busy city life but then something holds me back.

**Haresh:** Being amid nature can become a habit, and can cause addiction....

Mauley would have a faraway look in his eyes when talking about meeting people, his experiences with them, how he and they together made the impossible possible, and yet when they would part, the chapter would be over. Life imitates experiences and I was beginning to learn a lot about life and its ways from this bunch of enthusiastic people. Being a cycle otherwise doesn't allow you the privilege to ponder over issues beyond the here and now. But, the world of people is indeed large. There is so much to reflect upon, delve into and act upon. There are so many lessons to be learnt from one's own experiences and that of others. There are joys and sorrows, and one has to learn to exist beyond both, since nothing is permanent. Life, that way, is indeed a cycle. What goes up, comes down and what goes around comes around!

After about six long and gruelling hours of cycling, the four remaining cyclists arrived at the pass, though in instalments.

Atul was the first to reach, and the first to leave as he liked to maintain his own pace rather than slow down for others. Then it was Harsh and Gaurav followed by Satpal. And whoever amongst them had thought they were in the throes of adventure could not have imagined what awaited them thereafter.

As the three cyclists filled up their water bottles, mixed their energy drink concoctions, and ate a bit in preparation for their departure for the next leg of 30 km of cycling, the rest of the group was relieved that they were about to lose altitude. They were looking forward to the mitigation of the high-altitude and low-oxygen-related symptoms. That's when the five Tibetan drivers, through their Head Driver (one amongst them) declared a strike and refused to budge an inch. Well played!

**Head Driver:** We no move now.

**Harsh:** But why?

**Head D:** More money. Now! (Pointing towards the palm of his hands)

**Harsh:** What for?

**Head D:** For putting cycles on Land Cruisers midway to campsite.

**Harsh:** But this is already part of the package deal we have worked out with you.

**Head D:** I know nothing, we not move until you give 40,000 yuan.

**Harsh:** WHAT! Have you lost it?

**Head D:** You lost it. Do what you want. We no move.

**Gaurav:** Ok, let's discuss when we reach Peiku Tso.

**Head D:** We no move to Peiku Tso. Give money now!

**Harsh:** But can't you see we are tired? So many of us are sick. Don't you care?

**Head D:** I no see. I no listen. I no care. Money now!

**Gaurav:** But where will we run away from Peiku Tso? We are foreigners. This is a wilderness. We can talk there.

**Head D:** You take your bags out of the vehicles. You stay here. We go back, if no money now.

**Harsh:** Mauley, please intervene on our behalf. We had not prepared for spending that kind of money, and we have not taken any liberties outside the agreement.

Mauley and the others from the Nepal agency spoke to them and they relented a wee bit.

**Head D:** When you make problem, I call Super Head Driver at Nyalam. I talk. You wait.

While they waited, suddenly all the pent-up anger against their body's reaction to heights and against the hard stance of the insensitive drivers came out like worms let out of a can!

**Gaurav:** (In Hindi) Can you believe this? It is us who are 'making' problems, while these guys are the children of God!

**Harsh:** They have been briefed several times by the tour operators regarding this expedition, but it appears they have a fiefdom.

**Anita:** You know, since morning we have been telling them that one vehicle should always be in front of the riders, one behind the last rider and two in the middle along with the riders, but they refuse to follow instructions. They ganged up and moved together.

**Supriya:** And when we try to explain to them, they feign language difficulties.

**Gaurav:** When it comes to asking for money, there seems to be no language barrier!

After letting out a good amount of steam, the group waited with bated breath, as if waiting for the result of the talk with office management for a promotion and a raise. They were hopeful, but it took a call of barely five minutes to the Super guy by Head D to dash their hopes.

**Head D:** We agree to 10,000 yuan, no less. Money now (he again pointed to the palm of his hands).

**Harsh:** Now, you wait. I also need to consult.

A dejected Harsh came back to the rest of the group along with Gaurav and Mauley.

**Mauley:** Sir, few of these drivers on this route are known for this kind of fleecing. They will ask you for money under some pretext every kilometre if they can!

**Gaurav:** Never in my life have I come across such uncouthness!

**Harsh:** Now what do we do?

**Rajiv:** We pay, and lose altitude. They struck when it hurt the most. We have no choice now.

All agreed. They solemnly gave the money. Getting stranded and then fleeced at 17,500 feet, breathless, nauseous, feverish, and heads exploding with pain, now this was real adventure!

Harsh, Gaurav and Satpal decided to continue cycling and catch up with Atul, while the rest boarded the Land Cruisers. We cycles knew that the four cyclists were exhausted beyond measure. It was as if every ounce of energy had been sucked out from each cell of their legs and lungs: we could sense it from the amount of effort every single rotation of the pedal was taking. Like an avalanche, realisation had already hit the cyclists that they were not acclimatised for this; but standing on Nyalam Pass when they saw the gorgeously cyclable downhill track leading towards Peiku Tso, vitality returned as if it had never disappeared. It was simply a roll down for as far as the eyes could see. The view was stunning in its vastness and vivacity. They began to cycle us again, gloriously heading for the horizon, and saw no reason to suppose that anything could mar their ride. But soon enough, the carefree hands of nature began beefing up the weather against us.

It was close to minus 5 degree Celsius and the accompanying wind howled in the cyclists' ears as though practicing the background score of *The Exorcist*! As if this was not enough of a perturbance, after about 9 km, the undulations began again. This time, Gaurav and Harsh were quite clear that their bodies were not going to respond anymore to the requirements of the climbs. Thus, at this point, they called it a day and their cycles too were loaded on carriers and taken to camp while they boarded the Land Cruisers. Atul, meanwhile, had gone much ahead with the intention of completing the day's schedule. He was followed by Satpal, who at his innate slow pace, had also decided to test his limits. So barring Atul and Satpal, 12 members of the group reached the campsite at 5 pm, a stunning spread of nature with the Shishapangma peak watching over them, just short of Lake Peiku Tso. This was the first day of camping and the first day of acceptance that digital maps can break your heart and body.

As the Support Group hopped out of their Land Cruisers at the campsite, they soaked in the gorgeous dream-like surroundings with a generous spill of wows and deep breaths. It mentally relaxed them no end, though physically they continued to recuperate from the sudden ravages of height gain. Anurita, being the film buff she is, with a keen eye for visual arts, began seeing the place as one that Hindi film directors had missed out on tapping. Those chiffon saree-clad leading ladies of Indian cinema who prance about in locales across Europe had a much better option next door, she beamed to the rest. In the meantime, our four demure ladies forgot all about their harrowing experience on top of Nyalam Pass and immersed themselves in the resplendence of the shades in the sky, the greens in the landscape, the whites of the peaks and the gentle

***Level of Services detailed by Harsh: For Camping***

1. *The camp should be in a flat place that is sheltered from the wind.*
2. *If possible, camp should be suggested/established at places where there is a natural source of water.*

**For Tents**

1. *These should be three-person tents where only two persons will be staying in each tent, as extra space is required for luggage and preparation of cycling for the next day.*
2. *Tent numbers: Seven for group members, one dining tent, one toilet tent, one kitchen tent, staff tents.*
3. *There should be front canopy at the access to the tent for rain protection.*
4. *Tents should be ventilated but there should be option of sealing off the ventilation.*
5. *Tents should be waterproof from above as well as from below.*
6. *Tents should be set up on plain horizontal surface and not over rocks or inclined plain.*
7. *All tents should be close to each other with mouth of the tent away from wind direction.*
8. *Proper anchorage should be done to prevent dislodgement from heavy winds.*
9. *One sleeping bag with inners should be provided per person.*
10. *Staff should carry extra inners for replacement should some be soiled due to weather or any other reason.*
11. *A pillow must be provided for each member of the group.*
12. *Sleeping bags should be packed by the staff once the group members leave in the morning and again laid out in the tents once they are erected at the next destination.*
13. *Sleeping bags should be of the quality to provide warmth in subzero temperatures.*

murmur of the wind. They couldn't believe this was going to be the norm for the next few days. The long winding road alongside the campsite was intimidatingly close and yet the cosiness of the tents would allow privacy and comfort in this place they began to call 'in the middle of extraordinaire'!

Mauley and team got busy offloading, setting up the kitchen, dining and loo tents, the drivers of I-own-you-and-I-will-make-your-life-miserable fame had disappeared, and the women were hovering around the offloaded tents trying to figure out what to do with them.

**Swati:** Let's distribute the work. The cyclists are tired. Kumaril has fever and Anurita has a splitting headache. I will put up the tents.

**Supriya:** I will help you.

**Anita:** I will help Kuldeep identify the bags and carry them to the tents. I might discover my elusive biceps and triceps in the process!

**Anand:** Let me help you. I have regained my strength.

**Anita:** Before I start, can I have a sip of water from your bottle, Gaurav?

**Gaurav:** You can, but 500 yuan first! (Pointing towards the palm of his right hand with his left hand)

**Anand:** Which one is your tent? I have to put your bags in.

**Gaurav:** A thousand yuan first for giving an answer to that!

**Anita:** Gaurav, we are tempted to leave you behind in Tibet. After superseding these guys, you shall climb the rungs to become Super Head Driver, faster than we can say Tibet!

**Gaurav:** So here is Atul, our first hero, after completing 90 km of cycling!

The entire group went to receive Atul, give him water, and help him unload his backpack. He was tired but very happy from the effort. Kuldeep had got his camera out in preparedness for capturing the 'first look' of Atul and Satpal as they would get off their treasured vehicle! He caught Atul's exhaustion on film and then took the cycle from him to park it near the kitchen tent. Soon he was surrounded by the Nepali team with loads of queries about the timings for the next day, food choices, etc. Since Kuldeep was the only one who could understand their language, they felt close to him and had appointed him their mentor for the trip.

Meanwhile, Satpal was way behind still, cycling at a moderate pace. It was getting dark and I could sense that bit of anxiety amongst the group for Satpal's return now. Harsh was the most restless, less because he was the leader of the group, more because Satpal had to be chided once too often for clicking photographs by turning around on his cycle seat while speeding downhill!

In the intervening time, the ladies from the Support Group, finished putting up the tents, arranging the sleeping bags and settling the respective luggage inside. They were happy the loo tents were reserved exclusively for them. One may consider it utter luxury out there in the middle of nowhere to have access to a loo, but only as long as you have the privilege to be the first person to use it!

Anita crept inside her tent to settle her effects, only to find a young Tibetan shepherd, a complete stranger materialise from thin air, casually opening the flap of her tent and then sitting down on his haunches to simply stare at her. She returned stare for stare, not knowing what else to do. The staring match must have continued for all of five minutes when the young man finally smiled, perhaps to indicate that he had had his fill of sizing up the foreigner, and arrived at the conclusion that she is harmless. The potent smile of the Tibetans, particularly the women and children, is their only means of communicating with foreigners and making them feel welcome to their homeland.

The women decided to take a short walk towards the Lake before it got too dark. Just a peek at the Lake, they thought. They opportunely started but within five minutes beat a hasty retreat on being chased by local eve-teasers. You read that right—eve-teasers they were! Young local boys, tall and strappy, denim-clad, hair styled like Bollywood actors, cigarette-puffing machines, who seemed to be the officially proclaimed bullies of the village, decided to follow the women so close behind that they could almost feel their breath on them. They then tried to brush against them, comment and laugh. It was scary! Though now when I look back, I wonder why, for they were two boys unarmed, while our women were four: three of them in their late forties or early fifties and one in her mid-thirties (though I must admit that they still looked all of 18!), while the boys may not have walked the planet for more than 25 years. All that the women needed to do was turn around and scream, Bollywood inspired, *'Tumharey ghar mein maa-behen nahi hai kya?'* (Don't you have a mother or a sister at home?) It always works!

Unfortunately, the women in the group faced this age-no-bar-eve-teasing once too often on this trip and it left the group wondering if Tibet had imported this culture, or was it customary in this land to welcome women with such 'touching' enthusiasm. Or, perhaps, our ladies were irresistibly good-looking. Strangely, even the thought of being attractive was becoming increasingly frightening for them. And coming from Gujarat in India, where eve-teasing is almost unheard of, this was too much to take!

As they turned to return to the camp, it was already twilight; the setting sun was spreading the colours orange, crimson, scarlet, carmine, ochre, and even fuchsia. What a delightful show the sky had put up to make up for the earthy mistakes of humans! Just then they spotted Satpal rising and falling on his pedals, plying his way to the campsite on slow wheels and unwilling legs. What a relief and what an achievement! He was welcomed like a playful pup would be in a household full of kids.

The group decided that it was time they gave their complaining bodies a well-earned rest. A good 10 minutes were spent relaxing, before the clean air and the serene surroundings pulled them out again. One by one they began sauntering out of their tents. No one was about to waste a beautiful evening in the confines of a tent, except Satpal who was just too spent to heed to the calls to assemble outside.

**Harsh:** (Calling everyone) Meeting in the dining tent. We are celebrating Kuldeep's birthday today.

**Supriya:** Oh, wish we had a cake.

**Harsh:** Who said we don't? The cooks have made a cake in the pressure cooker with Nutella icing, if you please.

**Anita:** Pressure cooking a cake? That's a first for me.

**Atul:** Any activity that happens in the kitchen is a first for you, my lady.

**Anita:** I know. If I had just a touch of these cooks' talents, I would have replaced one of the three experts on *MasterChef* by now!

**Gaurav:** (On seeing the cake) Hey, these guys are good!

**Harsh:** Thank God for small mercies! Imagine if the cooks and the drivers were in cahoots.

They were all suddenly overwhelmed with ginormous feelings of gratefulness for the cooks! And Kuldeep was caught smiling ear to ear for the entire duration of cake cutting followed by dinner.

Harsh, who had earlier been exhibiting signs of restlessness, and therefore had gone quiet, unsealed his lips.

**Harsh:** We need to take the most crucial decision before we pick up our dinner plates.

**Gaurav:** The loo tent may not remain an attractive proposition beyond the first or second use, hence we need to split the landscape between the genders for the morning ritual.

**Supriya:** We prefer the area on the left of the camp, behind the huge rocks.

**Guarav:** Fine by us. So, the gentlemen may please restrict themselves to the right.

**Anita:** Please advise the drivers and cooks accordingly.

**Kumaril:** But there is flat ground on the right. How are we supposed to manage?

**Harsh:** By getting up before sunrise.

**Gaurav:** And what are your umbrellas for anyway!

When humans undertaking a camping trip in the depths of the countryside in Tibet, finally retire for the day, they snuggle inside tents, just big enough for two sleeping bags. I am sure that as they zip up the tent's door and window, they find themselves in a tiny little universe, cocooned from the chilly winds, the rain and the hail. It must almost feel like their homes!

# 11

***YUGEN***

***You-gen***

*(noun) Origin: Japanese*

*An awareness of the universe that triggers emotional responses too deep and mysterious for words*

## DAY FIVE: *Peiku Tso to Saga*

Somewhere on earth it could be raining, somewhere else it might be snowing, while at some other place the sun could be sizzling overhead like freshly made tea. But in Tibet, all this was happening almost simultaneously. Just one day of riding had revealed a very strange weather pattern here. Daylight would strike around 7.30 am; mornings were cold—humans would want to cover up every exposed inch of their body; by 10 am the sun would be rising strong overhead, but suddenly very cold, sharp and strong winds would begin to blow just before noon and continue until late afternoon. Temperature would range anywhere between 0 to 5 degree Celsius. It would start raining unexpectedly, and then, just as abruptly it would stop, and clouds would open to manifest the harshest sun; or we would be hit by a hailstorm without prior announcement. The weather is rather indecisive in Tibet!

We were at Peiku Tso. Even before the second day of cycling had begun, the prospect of cycling once again in the inconceivable environs of Tibet was already generating conflicting emotions. It was attractive no doubt, but equally daunting. Four cyclists were dead tired, one was down with high fever, and the rest of the four were not feeling too motivated either. Nyalam Pass had proven to be one big spirit-dampener. The original plan was to cycle almost 90–100 km a day, but given the difficult terrain and weather, the cyclists decided to rework their cycling schedule. They were quite clear that they were here not only for the challenge but also for soaking in the magnificence that is Tibet, therefore cycling more than 50–75 km/day would be a little foolhardy. The cycling schedules were reworked, and a total cycling of approximately 300 km up till Lake Manasarovar, was agreed upon.

The second day of cycling was from Peiku Tso to Saga. Fortunately for the tired muscles, but unfortunately for the bragging rights, the cyclists learnt that to reach Saga, they would be crossing over 60 km of utterly and uncyclably, broken roads. Here is what I have learnt along the rides. On such tracks, depending on the size of the rubble on the road, the cyclists may or may not land on the centre of their saddle. This can be rather unnerving. Therefore, in this life, a cyclist can choose but any of the two courses of action: he can either cycle on a wretched path and jitter his teeth and skeleton to complete ruin, or ride on smooth roads and give his body a fair trial and retain his teeth in the bargain! Somehow, the picture of the journey to Saga rising before the cyclists' eyes did not give them the requisite confidence to choose the former. Hence this day was ceremoniously declared a rest day, and we cycles were loaded back on the trucks. All 14 of them spread themselves into the Land Cruisers, four to one, a ratio that they dare not infringe, or be prepared to invite the ire of the Chinese.

Within a few minutes of starting from our campsite at 8 am, the group could see Lake Peiku Tso luring them. They could not have gone further without seeing and breathing it in from close quarters. The convoy was stopped, and they all began to walk towards the lake.

There is something about untouched nature, where beauty presides, that paralyses your reasoning abilities and reduces your brain to a window meant only for the exchange of good, clean breeze. At Peiku Tso, it is not just the animated tranquillity that numbs you, but the wide expanse of clear blue waters nestled against the sky, interspersed with hills that simply disintegrate you. The group, therefore, saw no reason why they should not continue to walk towards the lake, even after discovering that it might be a good 7 to 8 km downhill. In fact, they were hardly walking; they were running down at good speed, over what appeared then as the gentlest of slopes. As the cool breeze kissed them, the layers of warm clothing came off and onto the waist; the cheer and glee in their voices could have put an entire professional cheering team to shame.

As much as they showed their excitement, they went silent and ponderous too. Although metal outwardly, internally I have come to believe that we all come from bliss. The inception of my belief is a very interesting debate narrated by Anita, which took place between Adi Sankaracharya and Mandana Misra. Adi Sankaracharya was born about 1,200 years ago, and is recognised as the propounder of Advaita (non-duality) and the systematisation of Hindu philosophy. His contemporary, Mandana Misra, was a renowned practitioner of that portion of the Indian philosophy that was predominantly ritual based. Sankaracharya had perfected his philosophical beliefs after a great deal of effort and practice. He had adopted for himself the supreme goal of ridding the country of ritualism and unifying it on the basis of unadulterated self-directed spiritualism. With the intention of showing the gaps in Mandana's views, and to eventually turn him and his staunch followers, Sankaracharya approached him for a debate. To judge the debate, a person of a calibre equal to theirs was required. Interestingly, they both agreed that Mandana's wife, Ubhaya Bharati, was the best person to adorn this mantle and the debate continued for months. Here is a small extract from Pandit Rajmani Tigunait's book that I overheard Anita reading to the girls:

> **Bharati:** I would like to know what the mind and senses are searching for in the external world as they go through pleasant and unpleasant experiences.
>
> **Sankaracharya:** The mind and the senses are searching for joy and bliss, but they are looking in the wrong direction. They mistake mere pleasure for true bliss. And as soon as they realise their mistake, they are disappointed by the transitory nature of the sensory pleasure they have just received. Even so, they repeat this process hoping that the next experience will be more profound or longer lasting. But again, as always, they are disappointed and frustrated.
>
> **Bharati:** Why are the mind and senses so interested in finding bliss, or even pleasure?
>
> **Sankaracharya:** Bliss is an intrinsic characteristic of the soul. But in the outward journey of life, the soul has lost, or at least forgotten its intrinsic characteristic. And without the experience of bliss, human beings feel empty and dissatisfied.

And so on went the debate. Mandana, though stubborn about his views, was gallant enough to accept that Sankaracharya was more knowledgeable and his logic was a lot stronger. He was preparing to accept defeat, when the genius Bharati declared that the victory would be complete only if Mandana and his wife were both defeated. Bharati was accepted as the next learned opponent, but her very first question stumped Sankaracharya. She asked how a celibate who has no idea or experience of being a householder or a citizen claim complete knowledge of the universe. Sankaracharya was forced to ask for time out, to experience the life of a householder and reply to her on returning from the experience. She graciously agreed. When Sankaracharya returned, he was armed with 'complete' knowledge this time, and Bharati conceded defeat. Sankaracharya went ahead with his mission and defeated many a stalwart in the field of philosophy, to establish his system.

Coming back to 'my' philosophy, I consider 'bliss' to be like 'home'. However far we may go from it, even if for a few days, we yearn to get back to the comfort of our homes. Similarly, however lost or detracted we may get from it, we crave to return to bliss. We all come from bliss. That it is an integral part of us is evidenced from the fact that it never forgets to remind us to remain in that state, no matter what the circumstances. That very urge to continue to remain in the throes of happiness, had just taken over the group. The peace within was undisturbed by any self-created noise. It was just water, hill, the sky, the breeze and those 14!

**PEIKU TSO LAKE**

The sound of water
Not far behind
The flowers and trees
In the breeze entwined

A brilliant sun
Hovering above
With a lot of warmth
And a ton of love

All I want
Are moments like this
You and me
And the surrounding bliss

Unfortunately, the perfect harmony that had prevailed between man and nature was abruptly disturbed by Mauley's practical insight that the farther they went downhill, the longer it would take to get back. Somewhere midway to the lake, therefore, all decided to stop at a very picturesque spot, to smell the air, absorb the scenery, and capture the exquisiteness in their cameras. It was where it seemed they were closest to the lake. They posed and did all kinds of comical things for photographs, for somewhere they knew they were all by themselves, being watched by the lake, and unlike when being watched by people, not being judged for acts not befitting their age, experience and size!

**Atul** (Maximus photographer in the group): Anita, please stop, I am clicking the lake and you are coming in the frame of my nature photograph!

**Anita:** I am adding to your view. I too am nature!

**Anurita (to Kuldeep):** Have you taken enough pictures on the camera?

**Kuldeep:** Yours or the lake's?

**Anurita:** I meant mine, lake's, everybody's....

**Kuldeep** (with a naughty wink): I've taken some good shots of yours...the lake just happens to be in the frame!

**Anurita:** How funny!

Posing and photography over, they readied to begin the climb back uphill with the help of their trusted lungs and legs. Whoever said the slope was gentle must be a blockhead!

**Anurita:** At this pace, how long do you think it will take us to get back?

**Anita:** Doesn't look very far.

**Atul:** We are in the mountains, ladies. What appears to the eye will not be borne out by reality! Just climb, don't exhaust yourself by chatting too much.

**Anita:** Come on, Anurita. Tibet is testing us. Let us 'rise' to the occasion!

It took them an hour, and several thousand heavy breaths to get back to the cars. Even the extra layer of woollens felt a tad too heavy to carry on the person while climbing back. None of the Support Group ladies betrayed their thoughts, but in fact, the walk to Peiku Tso and back had led them to secretly question their levels of fitness. But one masks one's feelings when accompanied by nine people whose muscles (endowed so abundantly as to render the case of the Support Group hopeless) do not stop rippling even in sleep!

We reached the campsite in Saga at 4 pm. The drive through the circuitous and ramshackle roads was too much for the sensibilities of Anita and Anurita to take. The duo popped in an anti-emetic each and dozed off for most of the ride. At Saga, therefore, there were nine cyclists, three Support Group members and two zombies for the better part of the day. The campsite may not have been as fetching as the one at Peiku Tso, but nobody was complaining. It was indisputably better than the most stunning piece of nature they had connected with, in their earlier lives, in any universe.

Swati, as usual, took the initiative to put up the tents and everyone else except the zombies joined in to help. There is a certain something in working and staying together in the stark outdoors. It perks you up so amazingly, that the humans forget the existence of sundry horrors of modern times—cell phones, newspapers, television, laptops, iPods, iPads, i-this, i-that... which in their measly urban lives, seem to have a status higher than a good adventure or a stable relationship. They forget once too often in their mundane lives that nature has better 'connectivity' than all the Wi-Fis of the world!

Lunch was served at 4.30 pm and was followed by general lazing around and chatting. By now Anita and Anurita were sufficiently revived. Somehow whenever the four women of the Support Group got together, conversation veered around a topic that baffled them the most and therefore consumed them.

**Anita:** It has been two days and it is all quiet on my southern front.

**Supriya:** You know what will help? Deep breathing. And keep drinking loads of water all through the day.

**Anita:** But if we do that then the frequency of our requests for pee breaks will be directly proportional to the extra yuans to be demanded by the drivers.

**Anurita:** Not helping. And I think that the fact that we are going out in the open is messing with our psychology.

**Anita:** And to top it our biology is anyway messed up with our internal clocks ticking away at India time.

**Swati:** Try figs. And if that does not work, I have these herbal tablets that are a sure-shot solution.

**Anita:** How many figs? I am starting now.

**Swati:** Three. Maybe four.

**Anurita:** Hope that does the trick.

**Anita:** Eating figs, deep breathing and repeating...this sounds like sure-shot!

The Saga campsite was a lush green, vast, open space. The tents had been set up in a semi-circular fashion. During the day, the bright yellow tents against a vividly coloured backdrop of hills, meadows, streams, etc. looked like a hulk was being served seven egg yolks decorated *a-la*-Michelin-star menu on a giant plate. The humans spent a leisurely evening, washing their feet in the stream running by, lying in the grass with not a care in the world, and playing who-spots-the-best-place-for-loo-first. We cycles were given a good clean up by Mauley. Bless him!

Supriya and Anurita got involved in talks surrounding life issues—about God; what really is right or wrong, good or bad; varying perspectives and the like. Just then, Gaurav walked by.

**Gaurav:** Surpiya, give me the cellphone. I need to make an urgent call.

**Supriya:** Why, what happened?

**Gaurav:** You ask too many questions!

**Supriya** (tongue-in-cheek): That I do!

No matter where in the world you go, certain things about your disposition and communication never change. And more so when you are husband and wife! Gaurav, meanwhile, was helping Harsh confirm bookings at Lake Manasarovar.

After a sumptuous dinner of noodle soup, pasta, sweets, and yes, a cake again (Kumaril's birthday celebration), everyone crept into their respective tents by 9.30 pm, and within a few minutes, there was the silence of tired and deep slumber all around.

When you are in the middle of nowhere, with only a water-proof cloth in the shape of a tent separating you from the star-studded sky above and the green-brown earth below, with not a living being in sight other than the ones who are similarly placed right next to you, you sleep like you have never slept before. In the middle of the night, therefore, if you are woken up for something that is not even the tip of an emergency, what do you think will be the force of combined tempers? Exactly!

At 4 am when it was still night, suddenly there was a hustle-bustle outside the tents. The first two voices, bright as morning, from outside the tents were Atul and Anita's, and later 12 other cantankerous voices, from inside the tents, took off at each other.

**Atul:** *Oye,* get up everybody!

**Gaurav:** Why? It's only 4 am.

**Anita:** No, you don't need to get up and come out of your tents. Get up, as in, open your eyes and do a bit of work for us inside the tent itself.

**Kuldeep:** Okay, I am up. What is to be done?

**Satpal:** Me too.

**Atul:** I want everybody's attention.

**Harsh:** Go to sleep everyone. Tomorrow is cycling. We all need the rest. Atul, you too.

**Gaurav:** Atul, this had better be important, because I am on the verge of offering a reward to anyone who shoots you or shuts you up.

**Atul:** It is very important, Harsh; it won't take more than a few minutes.

**Haresh:** Okay, what do we have to do?

**Atul:** All of you, please switch on your headlamps and hang them inside from the hook in the centre of the roof of your tents, with the light facing upwards.

**Harsh:** Why on earth, Atul?

**Atul:** Because I am photographing the lit tents against a starry sky.

**Harsh:** You can't be serious!

**Kumaril:** Photography? At 4 am? A first for me!

**Gaurav:** Oh no, Atul! I always suspected you to be an eccentric, though in disguise. I hereby confirm it to the world.

**Atul:** Just do it. You will be really pleased with the results.

**Gaurav:** I am wondering if photography is your true intention and there is no hidden motive to torture us.

**Anita:** Even if there was, nobody can torture you, Gaurav, the way you can, with your sharp wit!

**Swati:** I have placed the headlamp, is that okay, Atul?

**Atul:** Yes, it is perfect. Rest of you please do it quickly, dawn will be upon us soon, and if that happens, the photography session shall have to be advanced to tomorrow night.

**Gaurav:** No way! Here, is this fine?

**Atul:** Absolutely. It looks astounding. And the photographs are unbelievably amazing. Why don't you guys come out and have a look?

**Twelve voices:** Nooooo!

*Jubilant at Lake Peiku Tso*
*Photo credit: Atul Karwal*

*The main street of Dongba—one of the most populated cities we came across during the journey*

*Photo credit: Atul Karwal*

# 12

***SOBREMESA***

***So-bray-may-sa***

*(noun) Origin: Spanish*

*The time after dinner spent talking to the people you shared the meal with*

**DAY SIX:** *Saga to Dongba*

We were to camp at Dongba on on the sixth day. By 9.30 am, radiant with an ablution performed to immense satisfaction, breakfasted, packed, loaded and ready, the group returned to the roads of Tibet with us cycles in tow in the trucks. Boundless horizons, with a generous scattering of mountains, hills, streams, untouched fields, and a lonesome Tibetan shepherd with his flock soon met the eye. Within 45 minutes we reached another pass. It had been decided that the cyclists would begin riding every day from the highest point on the route. Though the next 32 km would have their own share of uphills and downhills, psychologically the cyclists were assured that nothing would be as steep or high as a pass, and hence they were raring to go.

The group stopped at the pass, and then began the process of unloading us cycles and preparing us. Swati, meanwhile, was always the quickest anywhere in locating a loo spot for the women, and here too her detecting skills didn't disappoint. She climbed on to the highest point of the pass, and then climbed down on the other side for an undisturbed, unnoticed relieving. The rest of them followed suit.

The Tibetan drivers were hovering around the truck, not lifting a hand.

**Mauley:** Shall we ask them to help?

**Harsh:** Nothing in the world can induce me to do that. I would rather part with my energy and sanity, than with any more yuans.

**Gaurav:** I agree. Our capacity to take stuff and nonsense from them is almost non-existent now. Let them be.

**Anurita:** Thank God for Mauley and his team! The world may be full of opportunists but there are also people like them—helpful and easy.

Things seemed to be going on slowly, but soundly, when one of the drivers quietly joined Mauley to assist him in preparing one cycle. It was either their need to hurry towards the next destination, or the thick wads of yuans settled firmly in their pockets after being unscrupulously extracted from the groups, or just an outlet for restless energy that the male gender habitually suffers from between birth and death. One by one, all drivers joined in to help in assembling the cycles. Help notwithstanding, the process still took an hour. Despite the hard work, the drivers continued to show signs of being in a good mood that day. The iron was hot, it was time to strike!

Gaurav and Harsh called all the drivers together and spoke to them.

**Harsh:** We are cycling about 32 km today from this point and plan to camp at Dongba. We want you to go ahead and stop every 4–5 km, and wait for us.

**Driver:** Why 4–5 km?

**Harsh:** We might need water refills and other refreshments. Also for whatever reason, if any cyclist is unable to continue, they have the option to be seated in the cars.

**Gaurav:** And at every stop we would like to wait for the last cyclist, before we continue.

**Driver:** Who tell us, when stop?

**Gaurav:** Kuldeep or the ladies will tell you.

**Harsh:** And Anita is in-charge of taking photographs, so she will decide when to stop for photographs.

Kuldeep went down well with them, but the drivers looked with majestic indignation towards the women, and their expression revealed their utter distrust in their capacities to calculate distances. The ladies in turn completely disregarded the feelings of the yuan-gobbling drivers, and decided that they must start all good work with a toilet break.

Here is what they discussed at the loo point.

**Supriya:** How come this sudden change of heart in the drivers?

**Anita:** From being perfectly unbearable to a dash bearable, they have come a long way in just two days.

**Anurita:** Yes, but what a tedious pack! How come they did not argue at all today?

**Anita:** I need to understand this. I had come to believe that these guys far surpassed 'The Argumentative Indian'!

**Sanjeeta:** Even the argumentative Indian would use a great deal of tact and persuasiveness if he would want a glorious sum to be coughed up by his client. But here they are indulging in outright blackmail!

**Swati:** I think melodrama is a way of life with our drivers.

**Anurita:** They probably are the inventors of melodrama in the first place! I think we are getting used to them and their bizarre ways. Now if they don't do what they are doing and saying from time to time, we find it odd.

And thus, on a downright guarded note, the cycling for the day was cheerily flagged off from the pass by the Support Group. The cyclists gleefully plunged us cycles down the pass at full speed, the wind hitting us strongly while the horizon felt as though it was closing in on us. Before going downhill, we cycles always take the blessings of our brakes and commit our support to them. Without an effective brake system, one could just continue going down with no respite, and equally so in human life!

Having observed human nature closely, I can vouch the human mind is one of the greatest mysteries of civilisation. It is the sole cause of bondage and attachments, leading to conflicts, desires and greed. It is also the singular source of liberation leading to knowledge and wisdom. It is the mind that pushes a cyclist to continue riding even when his lungs and muscles are exploding. The mind prefers to take control of the external, rather than the internal world, simply because the former is more attractive due to the presence of the senses. For most humans to maintain an inside-outside balance, and realise that the external pleasures are but momentary, is tough, almost impossible. But we mountain cycles, take pride in noting that the cyclists that ride us, experience this feeling of detachment to the outside world of senses, to a lesser or higher degree, and sometimes even get a glimpse of their inner selves.

As the day's cycling began, the Support Group sat in the cars and began moving slightly ahead of the cyclists. They felt it was also time they learnt some basic Tibetan to communicate with the drivers. The strategy was simple, as you may be able to spot here.

**Supriya:** People here are so friendly. Every Tibetan we come across on the roadside or near our campsites calls out *Tah-she Deh-lek*. It means 'how are you', I think.

(That caught the attention of their driver)

**Driver:** Yes, that 'how are you'.

**Supriya:** How do you say 'Thank you'?

**Driver:** *Too-jay-chay.*

**Swati:** And 'Yes' and 'No' in Tibetan?

**Driver:** *Gong-dhah,* yes. *Ma-ray,* no.

**Anurita:** What about water?

**Driver:** *Chhu, chu.*

**Supriya:** For cycle?

**Driver:** *Kang-ga-ri.*

**Anita:** So a cycle here is equivalent to a female kangaroo! And for car?

**Driver:** *Mo-tha.*

**Anita:** For 'stop'?

**Driver:** *Kha.*

**Anita:** (To driver) Ok. *Mo-tha kha* for photo!

**Driver:** *Ma-ray*!

**Anita:** *Gong-dhah*!

It is then the driver realised that the dedicated genuineness and keenness the ladies were showing in picking up fluent Tibetan was decidedly not for cerebral reasons!

It turned out to be a good day in every way. There was bright sunshine all the way with gentle cool breeze keeping company; the cyclists seemed to enjoy riding us; Anita took at least a hundred photographs and what delighted the ladies most was that they finally knew how to get the cars to stop on demand. No more communication gaps there, feigned or otherwise.

On the way, the ever cheerful Kuldeep had taken ill; he had come down with a severe and painful case of conjunctivitis and fever. In the outdoors in Tibet, this is something that is caught easily. Anita, too, was feverish, and body ache gripped her like pedal and cleats. Well, they just had to wait for the return of their doctor-cum-tour leader, Harsh, for medication. The Support Group members reached the campsite at Dongba, about half an hour before the cyclists. By now they had got into the routine of arriving early to help set up the camp. As usual, Swati took the initiative to put up the tents, and the other three women joined in. The layout of the campsites used to be such that the sleeping tents and dining tents would be close to each other, the cars and trucks would also be parked nearby, and the loo tent would be put up at a safe distance.

**Supriya:** Where is Kuldeep?

**Anurita:** Not too well. He has been directed by Harsh to take rest and sleep a while.

**Swati:** One realises the value of following a fitness regime even more when you are outdoors like this.

**Anurita:** But until now, I haven't ever given it a thought. Be it cheese or chocolates, I never tell myself to stop until I feel like stopping. While we are still young, it may do no harm. But what's the point if after a few years, the doctor has to put an end to some of your favourite food. Oh goodness, I don't even want to think of it!

**Supriya:** Yes, old age is not far, and it may not always be kind in matters of health.

**Anita:** I keep thinking of exercising and sorting my present to ensure the future is smooth, and that holds true for so many other things too, but it is so difficult to discipline me!

**Anurita:** More than anybody, I think it is me who needs to either begin taking walks, hit the gym, or get into cycling mode.

**Anita:** There, you said it. Join the cycling lot. You don't know how gifted you are. You know how to cycle. I am a cipher at manoeuvring anything that has wheels!

As the cyclists started to roll into the campsite, Gaurav could be heard loudly clearing his nose, while Atul, riding right behind could be heard inquiring equally loudly, 'Hey Gaurav, is it raining or are you draining?'. Even though Gaurav seemed unmoved by this rhapsody, the riders looked like a happy lot. They entered the campsite, changed into comfortable gear, and within minutes were found lounging in easy chairs, eating hot noodle soup, and feeling delighted as if the beauty and weather of Tibet was their own special invention.

**Atul:** Doc, looks like me and my back are not on talking terms. And what shall we do for Anita's bodyache?

**Harsh:** Husband and wife to report to me here. I will give each of you a back massage.

Harsh turned out to be quite an expert at it.

**Atul:** You are good. No, that is an understatement, you are brilliant at it.

**Harsh:** Anita and Anurita, I insist that you give my complete contact details as a masseuse in the book you are planning to write on this trip.

**Anita:** Why would we do that? We feel it is perfectly fine to report you as a good doctor and organiser.

**Anurita:** Doc, you really can humour with a straight face!

**Harsh:** This is just to have an alternative career in hand for a rainy day.

**Gaurav:** Well, Harsh can take his pick for an alternative profession from a range of things he is capable of. You know, my bookstore picked up only after Harsh made a business software for me. It's been so many years, I still rely on that.

**Haresh:** Harsh made cycle rollers for me from machinery used in the pharmaceutical industry.

**Supriya:** So many people I know call Harsh over for a meal, just so that he can take care of their plumbing, electric and computer-related problems.

**Anita:** Why Harsh, why? Why would anyone do so much as to render the rest of humanity useless?

**Harsh:** But I am genuinely confused. There is nothing more complicated and bewildering in life than to choose a profession post-retirement, especially when there are so many exciting options!

**Gaurav:** There is, of course, something even more complicated in life.

**Harsh:** What is that?

**Gaurav:** Supriya has decided against allowing us to put our stuff on yaks during the *parikrama* of Mount Kailash. And so I am going to end up with everything on my back!

**Anita:** I know you are an animal lover, Supriya, but are you so sensitive about it?

**Harsh:** Sensitive? You cannot imagine the level! Once when their kitchen door got infested with termites, she did not allow it to be treated with anti-termite spray. She insisted that they be allowed to feed on it. When that door was completely eaten away and about to fall, that's when she permitted it to be changed.

**Anita:** Now that is truly, intricately and problematically complicated!

Soon, it was evening if you believed your watch, but the sun was showing no signs of retiring. In the evenings, despite the sun overhead, the temperature would hover around 1 or 2 degree Celsius and the wind would add a chill factor enough to ensure that the humans dressed like Eskimos. That chilly evening, one of the Tibetan drivers was seen emerging from his tent, shoeless, in a sleeveless vest, and trousers folded up to the knees, carrying a bucket of water and moving towards where the cars were parked. While the group chattered away in the cold, the driver began to wash his car lovingly, barefoot. The rest of the drivers too joined him in the same abnormal activity which they conducted on their respective cars. It was a relaxed day, but I overheard Anita telling Kuldeep that you don't go about killing yourself with freezing water to relax!

At 7.30 pm when the group sat down to have a yummy dinner of pasta, it was still not dark. They retired early that day, as they could no longer take the cold. Every night after getting into their tents, just before sleeping, they would follow the ritual of an inter-tent conference.

**Atul:** Supriya, I killed an insect under my tent mat. What shall I do?

**Supriya:** Why are you telling me?

**Atul:** To check date and time of funeral ceremony. Shall we have it tomorrow?

**Gaurav:** You do that any time, as long as you are not going to wake us up again for any tent photography in the middle of the night.

**Atul:** Okay, so if I don't call you guys to attention with your headlamps by 4 am, you may go off to sleep after that!

**Gaurav:** *Natak* (drama) Company!

**Rajiv:** Who is snoring?

**Atul:** Anita and I are still chatting.

**Kumaril:** Not me.

**Harsh:** I am awake.

**Anand:** Not me.

**Satpal:** My wife would have told me if I had ever snored.

**Haresh:** Not me.

**Kuldeep:** Anurita and I are talking.

**Swati:** Sanjeeta and I are awake.

**Gaurav:** And Atul is not letting Supriya and me sleep.

**Rajiv:** So who is snoring?

**Kumaril:** Could it be the foreigners?

Even though my 14 were the foreigners themselves, with conviction they assumed the Tibetan drivers and Nepal tour agency guys to be the foreigners here!

# 13

***SIRIMIRI***

***See-ree-me-ree***

*(noun) Origin: Spanish*

*A light rain; a fine drizzle*

**DAY SEVEN:** *Dongba to Paryang*

When humans used to urban comforts, have done their morning ritual in complete dignity and privacy, it is excusable for them to show some emotion. In the Dongba morning, all were beaming from ear to ear and life was seeming like a bed of roses. It was 7 am and the strength of the group, that is the cyclists, some of them already laden with buttered toast and Chinese omelette at breakfast, were settling down to the idea of a tough ride ahead that day, when the women entered the dining tent. They had that faint touch of bliss after a good night's rest playing on their expressions.

**Swati:** How is the omelette, Gaurav?

**Gaurav:** Will tell you in three seconds.

**Gaurav:** (After exactly three seconds with a determined countenance) Edible!

**Harsh:** Cyclists, Support Group and countrymen, lend me your undivided attention! We begin our ride today from campsite itself and we stop only when we spot a good campsite, somewhere near Paryang. So, we might end up riding more than 60 km today. Are you all ready?

**Cyclists:** Yes!

**Harsh:** I am looking forward to the sun. Guys, see this (showing off the exposed portion of his legs). I call this 'honour tan'.

**Kumaril:** It pains me no end, that a mere fever prevents me from being 'honoured' by the Tibetan sun.

Once again, they stepped out into the admirably welcome Tibetan sunshine for cycling and car riding respectively. The Support Group, armed with relevant knowledge of Tibetan, had decided to go ahead of the cyclists, and stop and wait for them at 15-minute intervals. At the waiting point, the cyclists would be fed some junk food, their bottles would be refilled, their dishevelled but joyous faces photographed, and then they would be given a noisy and merry send-off, before being met again, after another 2–3 km with the same ritual. Can you imagine how many times they must have stopped? The Tibetan drivers who had put up a love-my-car-will-clean-it-even-at-freezing-point-show just the previous evening, were understandably on a short fuse that day.

All through the ride, the girls I came to know were at their giggly best.

**Anurita:** I am glad about all the peanuts and *khakhras* we got with us. They really are coming in handy today.

**Anita:** Oh yes, the cyclists are having it because their bodies are in demand-mode with all that effort. We, on the other hand, are enjoying it for no good reason!

**Swati:** How would it be if we too were cycling?

**Supriya:** With no practice to back us up, that wouldn't have happened, my dear!

**Anurita:** It is funny how some things can seem scary even in imagination!

*Cycling in the hills can be mighty challenging*
*Photo credit: Kuldeep Jadeja*

*The late night photography incident at Saga*
*Photo credit: Atul Karwal*

**Anita:** Please live with this truth, girls. In the first place, it would not have accounted for the extraordinary time we are having, and in the second, two things rarely go together—gossip and cycling! And what would we do without gossip to spice up our lives!

More giggling!

As the day went by, the drivers of the give-us-money-or-we-won't-move fame became surprisingly mellow. Some semblance of earthy, honest humaneness had sprung up within the bunch and they were seen not just smiling but even joining in the laughter when the group chatted or cracked up among themselves. What more, they even allowed the women to use their cellphone chargers in the car. That was a first by any standards of kindness! Or so it seemed!

**Supriya:** That's quite a change of heart, I must say!

**Anurita:** True, can't believe they are letting me use their cellphone charger.

**Anita:** You never know when the old self resurfaces. Enjoy this while it lasts!

**Anurita:** Reminds me of how some characters in our Bollywood films have a change of heart. The world of films is as exciting behind the scenes as it is through the films we see.

**Anita:** I love the way you see everything around you as a film in progress.

**Swati:** You have been interviewing and writing extensively about them, isn't it Anurita? It must be a different world altogether.

**Anurita:** Well, yes. When they come to Ahmedabad for their film promotions and sometimes as part of certain high-profile launches and events, that's when they are interviewed and an article is carried in the newspaper the following day.

**Supriya:** They are not quite the way they are projected to be....

**Anurita:** Absolutely, in more ways than one. What most people see them as are these larger-than-life characters who have extraordinary lives. So, they expect them to behave in a certain way. They expect them to open up about their lives as if everything happening in it is for public consumption. Often people can ask them questions that can be insulting, hurting or irritating enough to put them off. But if they do withdraw into a shell and refuse to answer or even change the course of talk, they are held guilty! I think you require a good dose of sensitivity in dealing with people, be they from the film world or any other that has public access. I feel so glad I never had any bad or rough experience when interviewing a celebrity. That's because I never forgot that ultimately, they are all like us—human, with emotions and feelings that are no different. Would we like it if someone were to ask us something in an improper fashion? Or if someone behaves as if it is their birthright to know everything about us and our personal lives? I am sure not. Besides, if we want people to deal with us sensitively, why do we forget to give them in the same coin?

**Anita:** This world of glamour! I am glad I am not a part of it!

**Anurita:** True, anyone leading a public life for that matter. Our politicians, too, for example! We seem to be approaching our next halt. Will continue the subject another time.

**Anita:** Yeah, and next time we begin with some juicy stuff on Bollywood actors please!

I know journeys can be tiring in an urban setting, when destinations are concrete structures. But in the vastness of open land, man is a constant traveller, journeying his soul on flakes of supreme energy. As a cycle, I do not have the freedom that a human has, to create my own world. My world revolves around paths and everything that goes with it. A human's universe is humongous—both inside and outside. I wonder if they realise their good fortune, or they simply pass through life as a matter of habit.

The ride for the cyclists that day was like a lazy walk in the woods—enjoyable and well-paced. As we rode, we saw mountains and sand dunes at the same time. Like every other ride, this one too left me in a trance-like state. I suspect the feelings were mutual between the cycles and cyclists. In such smooth rides, it is possible for the cyclists to get into their innermost world of thoughtlessness and touch the ocean of calmness in that depth, which is nothing but the resonance of the exquisite nature outside. But for that to happen, a cycle's saddle and its comfort levels assume importance. Of course, in an imperfect world, it is not always a plain matter to obtain a perfect saddle; however, one must try. Most cycle-making factories claim that their saddle is built on the smartest of anatomical principles, but what they do not bargain for is that every cyclist's anatomy is not the same. We often lose our balance, if our cyclist is not comfortable on our saddle. In this group of cyclists, those who had brought their own saddles enjoyed the ride a lot more than the others. It was quite a lesson in 'rear management' (smirk) for the rest!

It took a while that day to locate a good, clean and scenic campsite. We crossed the Dara Monastery and Lake Dara Tso too (believed to have been manifested by Milarepa).

By the time a campsite was located, the cyclists had already covered 70 km on us. Though the site had a flowing stream and was close to the road, it had a waste dump nearby. Mauley

**THE LEGEND OF DARA-TSO AND MILAREPA**

Once Milarepa decided to challenge Naro Bon Chung, the sorcerer of Bon religion. In the battle that ensued, superhuman powers were exhibited by both sides, and it became difficult to choose a winner. So, they decided to race to the top of Mount Kailash in a bid to have a winner.

While Naro Bon Chung was advancing very fast with the help of a magic drum, Milarepa just sat down in meditation at the base of the mountain. Just before Naro Bon Chung could reach the peak, Milarepa reached there seated on the rays of the sun.

It is said that the defeat of Naro Bon Chung by Milarepa paved the way for Buddhism to replace Bon as the main religion of Tibet. When Milarepa was returning from Mount Kailash, he was carrying with him a huge block of ice and a towel. When he reached the point where Dara Lake is today, he simply wrung his towel and created this Lake.

and team had almost set it up, when the odour accompanying the cool breeze assaulted their sense of well-being like an enemy firing away indiscriminately from across the border. It was not long before they decided that they were not prepared to spend an entire night in the company of reeking solid waste, or for that matter even a few minutes. So, together they uprooted the tents, picked up their baggage, and loaded up once again. The cyclists rode another 22 km, while the others drove further ahead and finally discovered a greener, cleaner and untouched campsite. No smell. No dump. No junkyard. Nobody. It was just perfect. They set up camp and ended up having lunch only at 6 pm that evening. The tomato soup, rice, potato and peas curry and some dry fruits tasted like the meals that are most likely served in heaven.

Perhaps it was the combined might of the exhaustion of cycling and the stress of shifting camp that gave Harsh a migraine. The group couldn't afford to have their one and only doctor under the weather. Atul and Haresh gave him a good head and back massage and later claimed enough expertise to be listed as masseuses alongside Harsh, in the Hall of Fame, that is, in this book.

Just while the tents were being erected, three Tibetan women appeared, dressed in richly coloured silks, and dripped in disturbingly garish cosmetics on their faces and hands. They seemed to be casual passers-by initially. I even presumed that they had walked in from the neighbourhood to satisfy their inquisitiveness. Smart men on their mean machines could indeed be a draw! On getting closer to the campsite, they started gaping at the Support Group—at the four women with curiosity, but mostly at Kuldeep, the solo athletic member, with interest. They then studied some of the group's other men, tall with water bottles in hand, standing at a distance. It seemed like they were gauging something, question marks writ large on their heavily made-up faces. Purple lip colour and pink eye-shadow on one of the women was a bit too stark to merge with the serene earthy shades of the landscape. Another one, standing right beside her, had kohl-lined eyes that were screaming for attention, her nail-paint a bright shade of orange was both, brash and out of place. What on earth were they here for? Why were they staring at everyone, and finally settling their gazes on the men in the group? Why were they driven off by Mauley and gang? Well, I will never know, but I have a faint idea about this; and I am sure you do too.

As the sun was setting, Rajiv, Kuldeep and Anurita set out for a walk over the little bridge nearby. The iron bridge ended within a few paces of having begun but the view and experience it provided was unequalled in all these days. The orange shades of the setting sun made the place look so romantic! The stream of water beneath was singing a song only nature can compose. It induced light talk and the three stood on its edge.

**Anurita:** This bridge seems so interesting. Cantilever or arch bridge?

**Kuldeep:** Photo bridge! Let's take some pictures here... the light is just right. The photographs will turn out amazing.

**Rajiv:** Am glad we packed up from there and stationed ourselves at this exquisite campsite.

**Anurita:** I think Anita and the rest ought to see and experience this too. Such a cute bridge this is. It reminds me of my English poems from high school, John Keats and Robert Frost, somehow. There is also an old-world charm to this place—the scenic surroundings, the mountain, sky, pebbles, gushing water.

**Kuldeep:** You wish you had a book along now, don't you?

**Anurita:** Well, not quite. I'd rather soak in the glory of the place and later write a poem on the experience, if at all. Or perhaps just walk about...Long walks amid nature are an exercise in introspection for me. And, this kind of introspection might lead to change, you never know.

**Kuldeep:** So, you want to introspect?

**Anurita:** Yes, I wouldn't mind.

**Kuldeep:** But I will not let you. Come, I'll take you a little farther. The sunset looks heavenly. We must capture it against this flowing water! Or what are the cameras for!

As the trio returned from the walk, Anurita rushed to Anita to share the beauty of the 'Bridges of Tibetan County'! Anita and

Anurita again took a walk over to the bridge and a while later, went to the kitchen tent to see what the cooks were preparing for dinner. Just then the black clouds began forming over us. We could see the clouds emitting rain on a distant hill, and slowly proceeding towards our campsite. When the first droplets hit us, it was like being blessed by the heavens. It rained for the larger part of the night.

**THE PARYANG RAIN**

When the clouds
Float down
To meet the waters
Of the lake

And the shadows
Linger on
In rainfall's wake

When droplets fall
And quiver on my nape

I open my arms
For old time's sake

At dinner time, as the incessant rain hit their dining tent with ferocity, the group's discussions veered around the acute realisation, that while they were serenely absorbed with the environs, how little they knew about Tibet. For instance, they did not know about Tibet's cuisine, fashion, actors, singers, writers, economists, the names of their universities, their scientific organisations, sports, sportspersons, or any other private achievements. In fact, they could not tell the difference between a policeman and an Immigration Officer, a shepherd and a shopkeeper. But bereft of the internet, and near-zero communication with locals, with no tourist-brochure-being-thrust-in-your-face experiences, they simply had to rely on their own intellect to sense the place. Each one of them had already begun to nurture their own peculiar attachment to the place—slavish, wild and adventurous, mysterious, feverish, cool, tough, stylish, exquisite, even spiritual.

On retiring that night in their tents, the inter-tent conference began:

**Satpal:** My tent is full of mosquitoes. Any solution?

**Harsh:** Yes, I have one. You zip your tent carefully, then wear your headlamp and switch it on. That way you kill the rascals one by one.

**Gaurav:** But what about me? Supriya won't let me kill them.

**Supriya:** I told you what to do. Open the zip of the tent a bit and then shoo them out gently. Simple!

**Atul:** And Gaurav, the ones that remain in your tent are the lucky ones, for they shall be wining and dining on international cuisine!

# 14

## *BRONTIDE*

***Brawn-tide***

*(noun) Origin: English*

*The low rumble of distant thunder*

**DAY EIGHT:** *Paryang to Mayumula*

It took a few days to become noticeable, but one of the Tibetan drivers, Dawa, who drove the women's vehicle, had become polite. Early morning at Paryang, he was found assisting Mauley in delivering the wake-up tea to the tents. It was quite disconcerting for the group members.

That day the humans may have woken up covered in mosquito bites and mildly complaining, but the outdoors looked better than ever. The sun was playing peeping Tom behind the clouds and the breeze was thin and cold. Their tolerance for cold had reached new heights and they were all generally in high spirits on the penultimate day of cycling.

The getting-ready-to-cycle time in the mornings was hectic. First, the morning business in delineated spaces, next the getting ready for cycling and supporting the group respectively. A quick gobbling of breakfast would be followed by the application of sunscreen lotions to avoid tanning, very carefully like a ritual, with the help of tiny hand-held mirrors, which showed only one square inch of the face at a time. Next the parading of the sunscreen-lotioned faces before the rest of the group to obtain confirmation on the percentage of face and neck covered. Meanwhile, some would fill up their water bottles, while others would walk up to the road to click some more photographs of the snow-clad mountains, the sunny campsite, the stream flowing by. The kind of pictures you see hanging on living room walls or in travel magazines were aplenty here. And lastly the packing up and loading up.

That day, as laughter filled the air and the cyclists were raring to go, those who hadn't taken a walk on the bridge the previous evening went ahead so they knew what it was, that was making the rest in the group rave about! Anurita seemed to be the only one among the entire lot who dreaded the cold, but she felt more than compensated with her share of photography of the snow-clad mountains.

**Anurita:** There's something so magnificent about snow. It may blanket the mountain but is aware what lies beneath is strong and unshakeable. I guess trials in life, too, must neither affect nor alter your core.

**Anita:** Anything that does not kill me, makes me stronger!

**Anurita:** How well said....

**Anita:** Nietzsche says thank you!

We were to camp at Mayumula that night after about 50 km of cycling. That day, cycling had begun at 9.30 am. We cycles surrendered to the enthusiasm of the cyclists, as always. You see, we machines aren't given to tantrums. If oiled, cared for and prepared well, with proper checking of our road worthiness, we can run without a hitch. If a cyclist ever feels that his well-prepared machine gets stiff uphill, or after long hours of cycling, it is only his stamina to blame. In cycle parlance, we believe that the cyclist is fully and singularly responsible for the quality of ride he will get. The machine is equally capable of literally running away with the rider or unsteadily yawing itself in the direction of the destination—it all depends on the verve and vitality of the rider. The bonding between the cycle and the cyclist, and their love for each other, is reflected in the quality of the ride. This group of nine cyclists had by now become our favourites, not so much for their cycling skills (to be fair there are many a skilful cyclist these days, and our group was no exception) but mostly for their cheerful confidence about life itself and particularly in taking care of us before every ride.

The Support Group was as usual prepared with junk food and water, neatly packed in the rear of the car, in an easily retrievable manner. Due to his perceptible civility, Dawa had gained the Support Group's womanly sympathies for being just a side-kick to the main conspiratorial driver. He perhaps sensed it and would stop the car at a picturesque stop ever so often. Dash! They ought to have made friends with him earlier!

The challenge came later that day when somehow the women were unable to communicate to the by-now-transformed Dawa, to stop the vehicle. They had to answer nature's call, but despite repeated requests, Dawa who was drowned in the world of loud Tibetan music, continued to drive, unaffected, for almost half an hour. At some point of time when the women sensed a 'natural disaster' in the making and saw no ray of hope in softly releasing the spoken word, Anita gingerly showed him her little finger and bellowed '*Mo-tha Kha*' in a voice that could have stopped main battle tanks from firing. Dawa comprehended this universal unspoken finger language and in no time stopped at a gas station that claimed to have a public washroom. But in reality, it was only a raised platform with a hole in it. As soon as Swati entered there, she could see the night soil of a millennium waiting to attack her olfactory and ophthalmic senses. By now the women had developed an unbeatable loo camaraderie, and just a faint expression of disgust on any one of their faces was enough to tell the others, to quit the spot in question without further ado and explore beyond. Hence, without further exchanging any word or glance, the women marched together to a place right behind the so-called public loo, into the open fields, where no smell or sight had even the slightest potential of being horrific.

I am unable to reveal any further details of the animated conversation they might have had in the car later, because one, they had hardly any conversation that day, and two, even if they had, I did not overhear them talking about it. All I am aware of is that between the meetings with the cyclists at intervals, each of them would somehow get transported to their own little worlds. The day that they would have their first glimpse of Mount Kailash was just around the corner. The women that day were ponderously preoccupied with this thought...what would Mount Kailash be like? Is the sublimity of the mountain as infectious as they say? Will I be able to do the *parikrama*? Am I fit enough? What will I feel when I first touch the waters of Lake Manasarovar? At length, they reached Mayumula and their thoughts had already begun to drift towards hot noodle soup. I loved the fact that these women would actively cultivate an attitude of forgetfulness. I think that is the key to nurturing a larger and calmer perspective of life.

On reaching Mayumula, around 4 pm, we were greeted with a slice of Tibetan heaven; it was the most picturesque campsite so far. It gave a sense of being in a gigantic green space where you could roam directionless for days and not find your way out. At the far distance, you could see snow-peaked mountains in conversation with dark clouds that were about to find their way to us. A thin stream of clear, cold and playful water ran a few metres away from our tents; there was a handsome hill right next to our campsite. The place was so pristine, even putting up tents there felt as though Mother Earth would get hurt. It was pretty far from any urban setting, or an airport. I could figure that despite being pleasantly regarded, it must be seldom visited by people other than those proceeding to Lake Manasarovar or Mount Kailash. The cyclists were patting each other for bringing the group to this gorgeous spot, and I was just feeling good that they were feeling good.

**Swati:** Can't believe this is all for real.

**Anurita:** Can't wait to put my feet in the stream, and thankfully the sun is still up so we need not worry much about the cold.

**Anita:** And I am feeling intoxicated with the scent of the earth mixed with a bit of rain!

**Sanjeeta:** A perfect picnic-spot! There is everything here—water, mountain, greenery, rocks, pebbles, streams. How exciting!

**Haresh:** Kuldeep, I can see you are feeling adventurous, the camera just hasn't left you!

**Kuldeep:** Ah well, for living an adventure-filled life, you must also do a lot on the wayside. And the destination will surely equalise all the jolts and joys of the journey.

**Anita:** Where is all the philosophy emanating from Kuldeep? Has Anurita finally and completely happened to you?

**Kuldeep:** Ha ha... looks like I am drunk with all this beauty and a drunkard can be excused for being philosophical!

**World Within and Beyond**

Away from the world
Yet a part of it
When you feel entwirled
And yet adrift,
The sweep of nature seems tough to resist.

Part blue, part green, the shades a mix,
The mountain calls out, a plan you fix
Walk along or cycle to it,
Come back revived, come back fit
With a certain light that within is lit

Experience a power strong and true
Charged and bright, blessed and new.

The group quickly put up the tents, settled them from inside, and soon got back into the open air that smelled fresh as a baby post-bath. Each time they would enter a campsite and settle down after a long day on the roads, the group preferred to relapse into a state of animated stupor. They would take some position in the outdoors, either on the semi-reclining chairs or the grass, stay comatose there, and prefer to emerge from this state only when hot noodle soup would get served pre-dinner.

That day, however, was punctuated with heart-throbbing excitement, fortunately of a temporary nature. They suddenly noticed an overly excited Satpal and Mauley climbing up the hill overlooking the campsite, dragging their cycles along. Before I lapse into this tale, allow me to complete the character study of Satpal. He, of doing-things-that-none-of-the-others-would-imagine-doing fame, is a rare one. He would make equipment for fixing cycles out of locally available hardware, turn around on his cycle seat while tearing wildly downhill just to take a photograph, help load the heavy bags of all the members on to the trucks before beginning to cycle, and already half-tired enthusiastically cycle on the Tibetan roads. His chief characteristics though are a love for adventure and an infinite capacity to bargain in shops that specifically forbid discounts.

Now the hill that Satpal and Mauley were negotiating with their cycles was not exactly a walkover; it was of rather comely height and steepness. Once they reached the top of the hill, the rest of the group including us cycles were treated to a feat none of us were quite prepared for. First Mauley, and then Satpal, came rolling down the hill, hands-free on their cycles. Luckily, both didn't lose balance in what we hoped was not going to be their favourite sport henceforth, and even the loss of our balance while watching this, was only short-term. Satpal on emerging victorious from the downhill slide had one look at his audience, and knew he owed them an explanation.

**Satpal:** Good race, wasn't it?

The group, dumbstruck, had no reaction.

**Satpal:** I would have won it too, had it not been for Mauley!

Silence still.

**Satpal:** He should have got out of my way. It is disgraceful how people are so competitive.

The group had no reaction but jaws were hanging and eyes were wide open.

**Satpal:** Oh, alright! I know how much you enjoyed it, just don't blame me if I never do this again!

The assurance that no more such freak adventures would be practiced within their direct gaze ever again, had a transformational impact on the group, and they went back to what they did best at campsites: laze.

So far, the dealings of the cyclists with each other and respect for leadership skills that Harsh demonstrated were of pleasant nature packed with exemplary patience, but at some point, the sharp Tibetan breeze was apt to ruffle the placid feathers of communion. After reaching Mayumula, the simmering undercurrents of we-have-cycled-enough-for-a-lifetime-and-we-are-prone-to-go-no-further could be felt. Harsh decided to call for a meeting to decide the next course of action.

**Gaurav:** The meeting of the brave riders with the 'honour tan' is called to order. Our Chief HOW shall now take over.

**Atul:** You know Gaurav, you are our indigenous dictator!

**Harsh:** I know you are all exhausted, but we knew this would happen, didn't we? Now there are barely 40 km left before we reach the point where the local government bus takes us to Lake Manasarovar. I know the terrain is tough, the uphill climbs are particularly trying, but we may never come back this way again. So, what do you say?

**Anand:** I say that we continue cycling till the last point.

**Harsh:** You are an inspiration, Anand. I, too, would like to continue.

**Gaurav:** I am in favour of the motion as well.

**Atul:** I am in too.

**Sanjeeta:** Can we go back, say 40 km, and start from there to cover about 80–85 km. You know, that way we can earn some more bragging rights!

**Gaurav:** Not for me.

**Sanjeeta:** (Looking hopefully at each cyclist) Anybody?

**Harsh:** It is not logistically possible, Sanjeeta. It requires a huge amount of planning, manpower, provisioning at intervals, etc. to arrange for our cycling. To top it all, you know how the cab drivers are. I am tired of negotiating with them each time our plan changes by a millimetre!

**Sanjeeta:** Well, okay, I understand.

**Gaurav:** Back to our topic please. Is anyone else accompanying us for the last leg?

**Rajiv:** I am out. I need to preserve energy for the *parikrama*.

**Satpal:** Me neither.

**Harsh:** Kumaril is out. Sanjeeta?

**Sanjeeta:** No, not me.

**Haresh:** My cycling is over for good in this trip.

**Harsh:** It is decided then. Gaurav, Atul, Anand and I shall be cycling for the last time in this trip tomorrow.

A sense of relief swept over the five cyclists who had decided that they were done with the cycling, while excitement never left the four who decided to cycle the next day. Mayumula was taking effect on all of them.

The women of the Support Group did everything that you ought to do to absorb such a place—from taking a walk by the campsite, photographing the beauty around, stepping into the gentle stream, covering themselves in extra woollens and even remaining silent for short intervals. As night approached, and the cold seeped in, they decided to gather in one of the tents for a post-dinner talk that included every subject under the sun, but ultimately veered towards mommy talks. Except Anurita, the rest were already mothers and were sharing their stories from days when their children were toddlers and how beautiful it was to watch them grow.

**Supriya:** There are so many things you learn from your own children.

**Swati:** And the process continues not for weeks or months, but for years!

**Anita:** My girls have been my best friends, loving and naughty all at once.

**Anurita:** There is nothing more amazing God created than a mother. When you have no one, you have her. When you have her, you need no one. Well, to put it across dearly....

I was parked outside the tent they were chatting in. It really got me thinking. How lucky are humans to have mothers and fathers, two people who will always be there for them, no matter what. As cycles if we can feel so wanted in just those few moments that our rider holds us, cleans us, tends to us and sparkles us up, I can only try and imagine what parents can do for their children whom they produce and look after with more love than they have for themselves. Nature is magical and one of the best blessings of nature is to have loving parents and children. Everything in life comes later. I believe some people equate money with love, who believe that by getting their children the most expensive toy, bike, car, they have done their duties and proven their love. But the conversation these women had inside the tent really made me understand what genuine love is like. That night, inspired by the numerous conversations that these women have had and I have listened in, I did wish that in case there is something like reincarnation, I really would pray and want to be human. I want to feel the emotions the way they feel them. I want to be indulged in with love and the feeling that I am irreplaceable in someone's life. I want to love and be loved the way parents, siblings, friends and soul mates do. It is just a wish that I wish for today, in these dark but beautiful surroundings, somewhere closer to Mount Kailash than we have been all these days. I believe wishes come true when your intentions and desires carry a genuine cell. Mine does.

A little later, the women realised no matter how interesting their talks were, time wouldn't stand still for them even if it were on gunpoint. They would have to sleep if they wanted to be fresh and up the next morning. After all, cheering the cyclists while munching on the endless stock of goodies by the side was quite a job by itself!

# 15

***CYNOSURE***

***Sign-o-shure***

*(noun) Origin: French*

*Something that strongly attracts attention by its brilliance, interest, etc.*

Both, Anita and Anurita consider themselves seriously and severely mathematically challenged but will not let go of any opportunity to indulge in numbers, so long as it is the precursor to a fair amount of drama.

**Anita:** Even if we do not do the cycling bit, it will require us to take at least 10–12 days' leave from work and homes to complete one *parikrama* and one dip in the sacred lake.

**Anurita:** That's right. And don't forget the costs involved, and the on-the-spot escalation of costs depending on the mood of local drivers.

**Anita:** Now if I were very fit, and my fitness somewhat equalled that of a Tibetan, I might take leave for a month and complete say four *parikrama*s and four dips in a year.

**Anurita:** What are you getting at?

**Anita:** At that rate, it will take me 27 years to complete 108 *parikrama*s and dips. Will I get that kind of leave every year? Never!

**Anurita:** What's on your mind? Speak up. One *parikrama* this time should be good enough.

**Anita:** I am trying to say that working women were never intended by the universe to attain *Nirvana*!

**Anurita:** And how is that?

**Anita:** Because it is believed by the Hindus that one circumambulation of Mount Kailash and a dip in Lake Manasarovar washes away all the sins of the past births, while 108 of them will ensure *Nirvana*, the final liberation from the cycle of birth and death.

**Anurita:** Oh no! So, what do our kinds do?

**Anita:** Plan for next birth! And if you are born a working woman in that birth too, repeat the process of planning!

Mount Kailash, the holy mountain is considered sacred not only by Hindus, but also by the Tibetans, Buddhists, Jains, Tantric Buddhists, Bon followers, South Indian mystics and some other lesser known sects like the Ayyavazhi, etc. Hindus consider it to be the abode of Lord Shiva, while Buddhists believe that it is the home of three of their Bodhisattvas—Manjushree, Avalokiteshwara and Vajrapani. For the Jains, it is the Meru Parvat on which Rishabh, the first amongst the 24 Tithankaras, attained liberation. Tibetan Buddhists call it Khang Rinpoche, meaning Precious Snow Mountain and believe it to be the home of Buddha Demchok, Bodhisattva of Supreme Bliss. The Tibetans also consider Mount Kailash as a natural *mandala*, while for the Hindus it also represents the *yantra* (both

**Names by which Mount Kailash is known:**

- Mount Kailash
- Khang Rinpoche (Tibetan)
- Kangrinboge (Chinese)
- Meru
- Sumeru
- Astapada
- Deva Parvat
- Swastik Parvat
- Sushumna
- Ratnasanu
- Hemadri

*mandala* and *yantra* are metaphysical representations of the cosmos). Tibetan mystics even today believe the secret entrance to the legendary spiritual kingdom of Shambhala is in the mountain. The followers of Bon religion believe that this is the mountain on which the founder of their religion landed when he descended from the sky. Mystics from South India revere this mountain as the abode of Agastya Muni, a disciple of Lord Shiva.

Mount Kailash has been part of Hindu mythology since time immemorial. The great Indian epics *Mahabharata* and *Ramayana* mention it in glorious terms. Kalidasa, the famous Indian poet of 3rd century AD in his epic verse, *Meghdoot* (meaning *The Cloud Messenger*), describes how a person separated from his wife, sends a message of love to her through a cloud.

**Meghdoot—an excerpt**

*Enter from Parshurama's Kraunch door,*
*And move towards north, furthermore.*
*Ascend a little, along slope oblique;*
*You'll soon reach atop Kailasha's peak*

*Used like a mirror by daughters of Gods,*
*Embedded in a blue sky the peak shall prod,*
*When you settle on Kailasha like soft black kohl,*
*Or like milky white ivory pieces, or a big mole.*

*You seem like a dark blue sheet of wave,*
*Spread on the shoulders of fair Baldev.*
*Lovely you look, dear cloud, my friend!*
*On the joints of the peak, along its bend.*

*Bright peak as pearl, the playground of Shiva,*
*Holding his hands, Parvati roams as a diva.*
*Dear cloud hold your rain, no drizzle, no motion*
*And lie beneath their feet, like stairs, in devotion.*

*—Translated by Mrityunjay*

The journey of the cloud takes it eventually to the city of Alaka, near Mount Kailash.

Mount Kailash is a pyramid-shaped structure, four-sided, about 21,778 feet tall, made of rock and snow. It is a stand-alone structure in the region and is isolated from the rest of the Kailash range and other mountains by a deep cleft surrounding its base. This isolation and solitary location of the mountain can be seen clearly on a Google terrain map. The *Vishnu Purana* states that the four sides of the pyramid of Mount Kailash are made of crystal, ruby, gold and lapis lazuli, and that it is the centre/navel and the pillar of the world surrounded by six mountain ranges, thus symbolising a lotus. Charles Allen, in his monumental work, *A Mountain in Tibet*, describes it as follows:

> 'Even in the strictest geological terms Kailash stands alone, being the world's highest deposit of tertiary conglomerate—a vast pile of cemented gravel laid down in the period immediately preceding the arrival of early man and then thrown up into the sky. It has four clearly defined walls that match the points of the compass, and on its southern face a deep gully runs down from the summit, cutting across an equally distinctive rock band of horizontal strata. This is the mark that has earned Kailash the title of Swastika Mountain, and it is this southern face, emblazoned with its talisman of spiritual strength, the Swastika, that the pilgrim first sees as he climbs out of India. Kailash on the horizon and, occupying much of the depression in the middle distance, what was formerly one large circular lake with an island at its centre, but is now two lakes divided by a narrow isthmus of high ground.' (The two lakes Charles Allen is referring to are

the circular-shaped Manasarovar, and the crescent-shaped Rakshas Tal).

The mountain appears to have horizontal ledges on its outer side, which catch the falling snow to reveal a design of horizontal stripes; different shades of the uncovered portion of the mountain (purples and reds and browns) peep out of the snow. The snow on the peak of the mountain on the northern face naturally forms itself into a snake's hood (known as Nag Fani), and it is believed by the Hindus to be the snake accompanying Lord Shiva. The geometrically precise and perfect shape of the mountain has been a matter of research since long. Scientists who have studied the mountain unanimously confirm that the four sides of the pyramid strictly conform to the cardinal points of a compass. Russian scientists believe that this pyramid is the centre of a system on earth, connecting other mountains and mountain ranges, and have even suggested that it could in all probability be a giant man-made pyramid constructed by some intelligent ancient civilisation.

The devotees and believers do a *parikrama* of the mountain at the base of the peak. Hindus and Buddhists do a clockwise *parikrama*, while the Bon believers do it anti-clockwise. It takes three days for ordinary trekkers to cover the distance of 52 km. Some devotees, particularly Tibetan mystics and Buddhists, prefer to do the *parikrama* by prostrations, which takes about three to four weeks to complete. As a cycle, I can only imagine that the ingredients forming the humans who do this stupendous act must be a rare combination of perseverance and the highest degree of pain tolerance.

The peak of Mount Kailash is considered so sacred that there have been no recorded attempts to scale it so far. Even when one of the world's greatest mountaineers, Reinhold Messener was offered permission to climb the mountain in the 1980s by the Chinese government, he unhesitatingly declined. Not to be deterred, the Chinese government once again in 2001 requested a Spanish team to climb. Protesting this move Messener stated that, 'If we conquer this mountain, then we conquer something in people's souls.' Finally, due to serious international outburst against the move, the Chinese authorities once and for all banned the climbing of this mountain.

Manasarovar or Mapam Yumtso in Tibetan, located at a height of 15,060 feet, as mentioned earlier, is considered to have been created first in the mind of Brahma, before manifesting on earth. 'Manas' means consciousness and 'Sarovar' means lake. This lake, therefore, is also considered as the Lake of Consciousness or Lake of Enlightenment. Hindus believe that drinking the pure water of this lake or bathing in it is a direct route to heaven, landing you at the feet of Lord Shiva. Every pebble found underwater and in the lake bed is believed to be a Shivling.

**Manasarovar Mythology**

'About 15 miles across, the sacred lake Manasarovar is a lake "formed in the mind (of God)". In his *Himalayan Districts*, Atkinson quotes an account of its creation from one of the later *Puranas*, the *Skanda Purana.*

*The sons of Brahma proceeded to the north of Himachala and performed austerities on Kailash. There they saw Shiva and Parvati, and there they remained for twelve years, absorbed in mortification and prayers. There was then very little rain and little water, and in their distress they went to Brahma and worshipped him…Then Brahma by a mental effort formed the holy lake of Manasa…'*

Source: *A Mountain in Tibet*, by Charles Allen

Manasarovar is a circular lake with a circumference of 88 km, a surface area of 410 square km; it is among the larger and elevated (at 4,590 metres) freshwater lakes in the world. Some devotees like to do a *parikrama* of the lake too. For my group it may have taken three to four days to complete what locals would in a day! Four rivers flowing in four different directions—Sutlej (west), Indus (north), Brahmaputra (east) and Karnali (tributary of the Ganges that flows towards the south) arise near this lake. Strangely, even though the fresh water of Manasarovar overflows into the Rakshas Tal through a thin isthmus, the latter is a salt-water lake. The location of the two lakes in this manner is considered to be a representation of the pure and evil.

There is a fascinating myth about the lake. It is believed that if you camp by the lakeside in the night, you might just see some lights descending from the sky into the lake, for that is the time when the Gods, Shiva, Parvati and Ganesh, bathe in it. Many people have reported sighting these lights. My favourite 14 did not do the night camping, so they will never know.

The mountain and the lake together are interpreted in several ways by the enlightened. One version is that Mount Kailash is not only the centre of the earth but is also the symbol of the centre (or the Sahasrara Chakra, also known as Crown Chakra, supposedly located on the top of the head) of supreme consciousness or Lord Shiva in the physical being of a human. When the Kundalini (latent energy, female in character, supposedly located at the base of the spine) or Goddess Parvati merges with the supreme consciousness, enlightenment takes place.

Interestingly, it is possible to detect enlightenment by the appearance of certain symptoms. Deepak Chopra, in his book, *Synchrodestiny: Harnessing the Infinite Power of Coincidence to Create Miracles* says, 'According to Vedanta, there are only two symptoms of enlightenment, just two indications that a transformation is taking place within you towards a higher consciousness. The first symptom is that you stop worrying. Things don't bother you anymore. You become light-hearted and full of joy. The second symptom is that you encounter more and more meaningful coincidences in your life, more and more synchronicities. And this accelerates to the point where you actually experience the miraculous.' (Quoted by Carol Lynn Pearson in *Consider the Butterfly*). I am somewhat noticing the setting in of the first symptom in this group, for they were growing joyous by the day, without measure and reason. Enlightenment may be a distant dream for them, but 'the wave had begun to realize that it might be the ocean!' to quote Thich Naht Hanh.

*The best view of Mount Kailash is from Dirapuk*

*Photo credit: Atul Karwal*

*Blessed by the waters of Lake Manasarovar*
*Photo credit: Satpal Singh Chhabda*

# 16

## *PETRICHOR*

***Pet-ri-kur***

*(noun) Origin: Greek*

*The smell of earth after rain; originates from Greek word 'petra' meaning 'stone' and 'ichor' is the fluid that flows in the veins of Greek mythological gods*

**DAY NINE:** *Mayumula to Lake Manasarovar*

On the last day of cycling, the excitement in the group was more about seeing Lake Manasarovar rather than accomplishing 300 km of mostly uphill cycling in oxygen levels hovering around 50–55 percent of that at sea level. The rain gods had decided to mark attendance all through the cycling route that day by pouring down in sheets. The cyclists were not the least deterred; on the other hand, they welcomed the chance to cycle in the rain. The slope henceforth was gentle, the roads empty of other vehicles and humanity, except us, and at least one driver's manner was becoming increasingly benevolent (about the inglorious experience in the past with this driver, I shall not even stoop to mention). No one could have asked for more. It did occur to the women that the mild friendliness they were being subjected to by the driver in question could be in anticipation of the relief that he was about to experience as the group would shortly leave for the Kailash *parikrama*. But our ladies dismissed the thought as quickly as it had transpired. Their enthusiasm was not about to be diminished by anything or anyone that day.

As 10 of them waited at Horse-shoe point, locally known as Hor Chu (the last point before you take government-authorised buses to Lake Manasarovar; Land Cruisers or cycles are not allowed beyond this point) for the four cyclists to reach, they each were mulling over the languorous elegance of the landscape by frequently interspersing their daydreaming with long sighs. When the cyclists did troop in, it was a sight to behold. The four completed the last stretch of cycling 37 km in about two hours. As they reached Horse-shoe point, there was something so marvellously innocent, so engagingly infectious about their yells of joy, feet off the pedals and wild flapping of hands that everyone was drawn into joining their celebrations. Ten of them emerged from the rain-safe environs of the Cruisers and together with the cyclists performed a few jigs in the middle of the Tibetan road, with the somewhat bemused drivers watching on and secretly communicating to each other, didn't-I-tell-you-these-guys-are-mentally-unstable.

It was 11 am. Drenched and happy, the group offloaded their bags.

What happened hereafter is completely based on the beautiful descriptions that Anita and Anurita would give within my hearing distance on their return from the trek of their lives. They would be discussing how to document their experiences, while I would absorb and treasure every tiny bit of their account. I knew I may not meet them again; this book is my way of saluting the group's spirit. The point I am making here is that everything I am about to relate now is all hearsay! Even so, rest assured, Anita and Anurita may have their quirks, but they are decidedly not the kind to purposely misguide anyone within hearing distance. However, please note that since it is just the two of them that filled my days with their non-stop gushing, what is narrated hereon is obviously based on their experiences.

There is an extremely impressive building at Horse-shoe point, the Chinese government's Tibetan Tourism Bureau. As the group trudged into the building with their bags, dripping water all over the floor, they were greeted with the most amazing of ceiling heights, an architectural wonder. In this extremely well-maintained building, made more beautiful by the display of Tibetan handicrafts, what immediately and obviously grabbed their gaze, attention and emotions was the male and female sign for washrooms. At long last, they were about to experience the delights of a clean restroom. There is nothing like an outdoor camping phase in your life to put the joys of sanitation in perspective.

They made a beeline towards the loos, following the arrows to the rear corner of the building, only to be greeted once again with a gas chamber. This posh looking building had the same 'hole in the ground' loo that they had earlier encountered at a gas station. Is it too much to expect from a progressive country to provide proper restrooms for the peace of mind and body of the tourists at least in their posh tourism offices? Or, has it not occurred to them that there is a better way of constructing washrooms? We cycles would never know. The group in their extreme disappointment decided to henceforth give up on expecting anything even close to hygiene and sanitation for the rest of their trip. I think that was wise!

I observed these people didn't mull over anything for long. With people like Gaurav, Harsh, Atul, Rajiv, Kuldeep and Kumaril amongst them, whose brains are wired to locate the fun factor in everything, they were never faced with the loss of their sanity or patience for more than a moment. As they waited in the huge lounge of the Tourism Bureau for the Chinese bus service to serve them a bus for their road trip to Manasarovar, laughing over silly jokes, they gorged on chocolates and dry fruits. This, evidently, in celebration of completing cycling and in preparation for the tough trek ahead, but in fact simply out of a longing for bad cholesterol and excessively sugar-laden food. Occasionally, they also spoke and behaved as though it had been ages since they saw, encountered or entered a concrete structure.

Just as the clock struck noon, the arrival of two buses of the Tibet Tourism Company Ltd was announced. In addition to our 14, another 20–25 passengers had gathered by now, mostly Tibetan/Chinese and a few Europeans. They stood loosely scattered around the bus, but not in a perfect queue, as was the case earlier at Nyalam. It was strange to find that this place did not have the kind of security that they had witnessed ever since their entry and throughout their trip in Tibet. Gratified though they were that there were no gun-toting Chinese policemen staring their self-esteem down (for they had begun to feel like illicit liquor in their presence), they were mentally already transported to a more elevated state of being, in anticipation of the first view of the grand lake and the majestic mountain. The bus was brimming with modern comforts and the driver directed a genuine smile at them (you know the kind that reaches from ear to ear) and genially helped in loading their bags. Life in Tibet can surprise you when you least expect it!

It was a ride of almost 70 km to Chiu Gompa monastery which is perched on a hill overseeing Lake Manasarovar. They drove in silence. I am told this place is so magical that if you were to die here, you would hate to utter your last words, lest you disturb the delicate silence that embraces you all around.

The real Tibetan plateau could be seen here—flat landscape, variegated colours of the earth, sparse vegetation, drooping skies, cloudy and windy, clean sharp air; it was a fulfilling experience in every way. A few kilometres ahead of their destination, the driver announced he would stop to show them a view to die for. And when he did stop at a vantage point, bless him, the group was rewarded with the sight of two of the most beautiful lakes in the world. Located on either side of the hill where they stood, literally spilling cool blue water on their delighted senses, were the Lake Manasarovar and the Rakshas Tal, both as stupendous, both as calming, both as heavenly. Among the many mysteries of nature, the rendition of perfect water bodies at even more perfect locations never ceases to astonish.

The first view of the lakes, though from a distance, left them totally breathless, and almost irretrievably lost. They must have stood there for a long time, some of them attempting to etch the vision in their memories, while others absorbing the view with the assessing gaze of someone about to plunge into the lake water. Soon, Mr. Ear-to-ear-smiles softly called out to board the bus. They could tear themselves away only because they knew they were headed straight to Lake Manasarovar.

In another half hour, they reached the banks of 'the' lake. The bus stopped, and they found themselves in the most amazingly electrifying place on earth; Lake Manasarovar stretched right before them—blue, placid and inviting. The rest of the setting

**LAKE MANASAROVAR**

Quiet and still<br>
Deep and blue<br>
Distant hill<br>
Ethereal hue

As thought-free I<br>
Absorb this view<br>
I live or die<br>
It matters few

Though every life<br>
Shall end in death<br>
What matters more<br>
How I lived each breath

So here I stand<br>
Quiet and still<br>
Breathing in<br>
Water and hill.

was punctuated at distant intervals by the hill containing Chiu Gompa monastery, few other hills far in the horizon, and a few motels close by. In some kind of a daze they unloaded, and then half-carried, half-dragged their bags to the tiny motel they were booked in.

The motel had a beautiful view of the lake, and that is what helped the group overlook its dingy, unclean and unkempt interiors. The motel comprised of four microscopic rooms with creaking beds placed leg-to-leg on the floor and edge-to-edge with the walls. The ceilings closed on you as if waiting to take a swipe at you. Unruffled by the lack of amenities, whatever delusion they were labouring under with regard to the motel, it was further enhanced by the idea that it was located barely 50 metres from the lake. And for that our group was ready to give this place an A+ rating.

On entering and settling in their rooms, there was boundless excitement for reasons that urban dwellers might fail to appreciate, but tent occupants can identify with.

**Kumaril:** For the first time in a week, I will enter my sleeping space without contorting my body and bending low. I have just realised how much I love the doors in our homes and offices.

**Harsh:** We can change clothes while standing; what a relief!

**Rajiv:** So much easier looking for stuff in your bags. Packing and unpacking made easier.

**Anita:** Thank you, high ceilings! I am ever grateful to you. How can I ever repay you for standing tall above my head!

**Supriya:** And it can rain as hell, but we can sleep through, as water won't seep in.

**Anurita:** We can take easy turns when sleeping and our legs can rest free. No chaining up, no stuffing ourselves in sleeping bags!

**Swati:** And all the girls will be together in the same room for the first time in the trip.

**Anita:** Imagine the amount of gossiping we can do about all the people we have never met!

**Atul:** Gossip later. Let's go to the lake and take a dip.

Anita loved to express herself in a theatrical fashion from time to time, often with the appropriate rolling of her eyes and hand gestures to go with it. But Atul knew that if Anita got chatty, she becomes like a rock, difficult to budge, hence as her conversation was about to take off, right in the midst, he dropped the idea of a dip in the lake.

Having seen Atul from close quarters during the cycling days, the one thing I realised was that despite his almost five decades of walking on earth, his power to make others feel and enjoy nature with childlike fervour was only growing. Anita knew better than most, that at such moments, when Atul would lend the weight of his adventure-seeking personality behind a mere invitation to take a dip in a lake, it could end up only in one way: by each one of them taking a dip in the lake.

Harsh turned out to be that rare exception who remained unaffected. The rest had come prepared for this; each of them had some form of swimming or water-dipping gear. The women were confined to one room and had a field time cracking jokes at each other's posterior and anterior while changing into swim gear. It somehow got them closer. I guess it made sense. We cycles, too, tend to get close to each other through intimate exchanges of creaking sounds that get louder with cyclists who are literally 'widespread'.

Atul got into the lake first, followed by Kuldeep; they neither yelled about how cold the water was nor shivered or chattered their teeth. The rest just felt reassured enough to enter. At the first instance of water touching skin, they were yelling with joy and the pain that the icy coldness of water brings.

Atul and Kuldeep had totally fooled them into entering God's own bathing tub, that was freezing beyond their tolerance limits, and yet they couldn't help being grateful. They, in fact, felt blessed. There were several other groups of people on the lakeside strolling and watching them with a healthy mix of awe, envy and amusement, but none of them ventured for a dip. While 13 of them splashed around, slipped on the sandy bottom of the lake and took turns in going underwater, Harsh sat on the beach taking photographs, watching them and entertaining himself by meditating on life I suppose. Or, who knows, maybe he was reflecting by force of habit, on the next course of action, as the group leader of this trip. Meanwhile, Satpal, for whom the world is nothing but a photo-worthy place, used his unique powers to repeatedly go in and out of the freezing cold lake, toiling to take videos and photographs of the group in their insuppressible excitement.

**Anurita:** Watch out, the camera will fall into the lake and that might be the only memory we will go back with!

**Satpal:** Oh don't worry, I am used to this.

**Anita:** Burr...the water is so cold...I feel acutely alive!

**Supriya:** Isn't it brilliant we are finally in Manasarovar!

**Anurita:** Yes, Supriya, I am now recalling our pre-expedition meets where your expressions were devoid of all the joyous enthusiasm we are now witnessing.

**Swati:** So, this is what we were headed for...so vast and amazing.

**Kuldeep:** Are you all enjoying?

**Swati:** Oh yes, we are. You don't seem to want to leave the lake though.

**Anurita:** Hmm. Well, I think all sins, if at all, have been washed off. We must now step out and dry ourselves, may be walk by the lake.

**Anita:** And breathe like never before!

As they returned and settled down to a hot lunch of rice, pulses and vegetables, you couldn't have thought that something as conspicuous as the Tibetan restaurant right next to their motel, could escape their attention, but it had, until now. The choice that they were presented with now was either to do their daily dose of lazing and lounging at the newfound restaurant, or pack up for Darchen, their next stop. They decided to do both in their own sweet time. The packing bit was a confusing, long-drawn affair. From Darchen onwards, they planned to carry small duffle bags and leave the rest of their stuff behind. It was some experienced Kailash-Manasarovar *yatris* who had warned them to carry their belongings only in duffle bags from this point on. It is very difficult, almost impossible, to carry the likes of wheeler suitcases and other fancy bags on yaks.

**Harsh:** So now we shall have to repack, such that we share one duffle bag between two people. Judging by the complication this is likely to cause, just to simplify things, tent partners should share a duffle bag each.

**Kumaril:** Neither me nor Satpal has a large enough duffle bag.

**Atul:** Anita and I have one each; we are pleased to offer one to you.

**Kumaril:** It is indeed an honour and do not worry; I shall guard it with my life!

**Anurita:** Where do we leave the extra bags?

**Harsh:** We will leave them back at Darchen, and collect them on our return from the *parikrama*.

**Gaurav:** I have completely unpacked all my stuff on the beds in our room and now that Atul and Harsh have done the same, I think our stuff is getting mixed up.

**Atul:** Hey Gaurav, did you see my woollen socks?

**Gaurav:** There, what did I tell you?

**Haresh:** I have laid down all the snacks, still unopened, on the dining table. Help yourself people.

**Kumaril:** I am about to do the same. My wife has packed snacks for me as though I were going to the moon.

**Atul:** It's a good idea to travel as light as possible. The *parikrama* is difficult, particularly on the second day. So, plan for carrying as little as possible on yourself.

**Harsh:** I suggest that we bid a silent farewell to everything that has outlived its utility. I am giving away my pillow and certain other stuff to Mauley and team.

**Atul:** Good idea, I will give away my extra pair of shoes and Anita's floaters and all her extra clothes.

**Anita:** I thought I was to be consulted before you gave away my belongings.

**Atul:** How many points do I lose this time?

**Anita:** Minus five billion points for not consulting but plus 10,000 for thinking of others!

**Kumaril:** What are these points for?

**Atul:** For my performance as a spouse!

And so it went on, until they were packed and ready to leave any minute for a trip that in reality they were to undertake only after 24 hours!

It was time for the girls to casually stroll outside and to act as if missing the remaining sunshine of a bright Tibetan day would be sacrilege, while what they were really doing was 'spot finding'. As they began looking around, they came across local Tibetan children with the seams of their trousers opened at the right place from the rear to the front, to enable them to hygienically and effortlessly perform ablutions. The poverty and lack of water and sanitation facilities is striking in this place.

As for the ladies in this story, due to the buildings in this area, they were presented with a choice of plenty: there were several open places shielded by the boundary walls of the buildings and there was, of course, the gas chamber. But what intrigued them to no end was that they never came across other women like them looking for spots to do their private business. There were European, Chinese and Tibetan women along with them on the bus. They even saw some Indians strolling on the sands next to the lake. Unless they had mutated to develop systems that let out stuff through sweat and breath, they had to go somewhere. This became the topic of the girls' extremely giggly and animated gossip.

It was Supriya who first noticed the clouds at a distance clearing to reveal what they had only imagined or seen in photographs—the peak of Mount Kailash. Just behind a string of hills, all that could be seen was the top portion of the mountain, golden with the rays of the setting sun. The sky embraced by the colours of dusk was blushing with splendour. The energy in the moment could already be sensed, it was as if permeating the core, and partly, it was to do with the glowing radiance of the mountain. If you have seen how the first sunlight after heavy rains will have enough intensity to make everything in the surroundings—trees, gardens, lakes, buildings, cars, and cycles—simply glow with an arresting sparkle, then you will know what is meant to be conveyed here. It was as if pure, undiffused light was emanating from the mountain and directly reaching to warm all hearts. In such moments of warmth and glow, perhaps everyone and everything simply inches a bit closer to their Creator.

The group returned that evening to spend some time in the restaurant, but the heavy odour of yak butter and meat drove them right back to their rooms. After an early, slurpy and noisy (they were so happy to be here that they could not stop talking) dinner, in a state of considerable satisfaction and joy, they called it a day. And ah! What a day it had been!

# 17

## *RESFEBER*

***Rees-fee-bur***

*(noun) Origin: Swedish*

*The tangled feelings of fear and excitement before a journey begins*

**DAY TEN:** *Manasarovar to Darchen*

Everyone slept well that night at Manasarovar. They wished each other 'good morning' in loud singsong voices, in consonance with the dazzling ambience. One would not be too far off the mark if one mistook their chirpiness for a case of complete evacuation, clean insides and consequently a certain lightness in step and outlook. They were to leave for Darchen later in the day, but right now the monastery overlooking Lake Manasarovar beckoned.

The hill on which Chiu Gompa monastery is located did not look terribly challenging; it did rise above others but not at great length. The soft cloak of clouds it wore gave it that element of enigmatic grandeur that couldn't have failed to attract any passerby. Anita, Anurita, Swati, Supriya, Kuldeep and Rajiv led by Harsh, Gaurav and Atul, began the climb towards the monastery as the wind tried its best to pierce them, through the several layers of clothing. With low oxygen levels, even a gentle slope felt dangerously elevated. The breathlessness of the climb provoked a barrage of questions that were shot at Atul by Anita: you have done the Mount Kailash *parikrama* earlier; is it tougher than this; is the climb gentle or steep; is it only uphill all the way to Dolma La; are my warm clothes enough;

am I fit enough? Atul simply smiled a patient smile and looked at her with whatever love and worship he could garner at that height. Anita had been repeatedly asking him about this, but wiser over the years, Atul knew that you don't ever, ever reply to your wife twice on the same question. If your answer differs by a nanometre, you are likely to be guillotined!

On the other hand, although the youngest in the group, Anurita and Kuldeep were wondering if their otherwise energetic selves would contain the energy for the *parikrama*. Kuldeep, who had been in the waters of Manasarovar for the longest patch, had begun to have a running nose. Being strong and rugby-built, he wasn't one to fall weak on the energy chart but if there was anything he seemed to have a problem with, it was ice-creams and cold water! What worked for him, always, was his warm disposition and easy-going attitude. But Anurita felt it was the same easy-going attitude that sometimes made him a bit careless about himself.

**Haresh:** He's our tough guy, all will be fine.

**Kuldeep:** Oh yes, we must look forward to the trek now.

**Kumaril:** I know…all these days have finally led us up till here.

**Anurita:** The fact that we reached up till here was only the will of God. Whatever will happen will be good and as per His wish. There is no point fighting it but yes, it is important we look after ourselves now more than ever. If nothing else, we shouldn't be a liability to anyone in our group.

The group soon found themselves at the monastery which was a serene picture of yesteryears, where the careless hands of time had not been able to wipe away the edifice of a monument built

*At Yam Dwar, you get over the fear of death*

*Photo credit: Rajiv Popli*

*The trek from Yam Dwar to Dirapuk is dotted with the bounties of nature*

*Photo credit: Kuldeep Jadeja*

only to embed utter silence and unbound peace. The group entered it from the rear side and walked straight into a dark prayer room. In fact, side by side, there were three prayer rooms, each with their own prayer altars systematically decorated with butter lamps. These were the only source of light inside. The walls were like a palette of unhindered colours depicting Buddhist paintings interspersed with *thankas*, and the air hung around with a deep sense of ancient history. You really had to make an effort to see the paintings in the dark rooms. I wonder what all that silence and peace must have done to the rough and tumble temperament of the cyclists.

As the group came out of the monastery from the front door, feeling almost connected to the antiquity of it all, the rewarding view of Lake Manasarovar from the top of the hillock, and a hairy and cuddly dog curled up in sleep at the door, brought them back to the brilliant present. Dogs are aplenty in this region: hairy, sumptuous, friendly, scary, sleepy, playful, wild, brown, black, and beige. Tibetan Mastiff, Lhasa Apso, Tibetan Terrier, Tibetan Spaniel, Shih Tzu are the better-known dog breeds of Tibet, but what they saw were the strays, no less attractive than the pedigreed. Supriya and Kuldeep, who is also fond of dogs, had a feast observing this one prance about and follow them here, there and everywhere!

From the monastery Anita and Anurita headed back to the lake. They sat on the ground next to the water just to be with the lake and feel its energy. It was not long before Anurita noticed the tiny pebbles in vivid colours strewn all around in the sand on the lakeside. In her excitement at chancing upon this fine detection, she almost decided to stay back at Manasarovar permanently. She loved it and started sieving the sand and placing identically shaped, sized and coloured pebbles in a row on the ground.

**Anita:** What are you doing with these tiny nuggets?

**Anurita:** I really don't know. They are startlingly beautiful colours, I am mesmerised at the wonder nature is. Maybe I can design some jewellery or trinkets with them. Imagine wearing Manasarovar on one's body! It can't get better than that, right?

**Anita:** What a lovely thought! Let me help you find some. Look, I found two similar ones that seem like garnets.

**Anurita:** And look at these green ones; never seen such colours before.

**Anita:** (Looking up to the sky) Hey there, no better artist than you!

**Anurita:** Can you hear the gentle sound of the water of the lake?

**Anita:** Yes, it is as if this poignant music is being played especially for us. Is it communicating with us, do you think?

**Anurita:** Possibly yes. . .God has His ways!

The duo spent close to two hours beside the lake. After Anurita left for the room, Anita continued to sit there, watching the stillness and the beauty of the lake, taking it all in. An air of soulful tranquillity suffused the scene. Just watching the surface of the lake waters being gently touched by the breeze, and breathing it all in, felt like meditation. She probably sat there for an hour, alone and happy, when the boys—Atul, Gaurav, Kuldeep, Satpal and Haresh—passed by cheerfully informing her that they intended to go to the far end of the lake. Anita continued sitting there, but this time she was watching the antics of the five guys as they stepped into the waters just to feel the cold seep in, and it still felt like meditation. Manasarovar surely takes hold of your consciousness!

After lunch, they took off for Darchen. It was a 40-km, bone-shaking, teeth-chattering and head-lolling bus ride, but the weather and the scenery outside were huge enough distractions from the distress. Darchen is a tiny town but is abuzz with tourists as it is the one and only starting point for the *parikrama* of Mount Kailash. Life so far in Tibet may have offered few chances of comfort and hygiene to the group, but Darchen was surely not one of them. The motel was structured like a train, with coach-like rooms. These rooms were larger than the ones at Manasarovar but the stench of months, if not years of unwashed linen, uncleaned rooms and rotting wood was overwhelmingly powerful to be ignored. Anita was the first to enter the room allocated to women. She had barely taken her first step in, when she shot out of the room like a cannon, filled with a sense of unease, somewhat like what she had been experiencing with the loos. But then, that was before Swati discovered the shanty with a hole in the ground at the same motel that was respectfully addressed as the 'loo'.

The rooms were dormitory-like, that had been used and overused by previous travellers. The moteliers seemed to be having a running battle with doors. Neither could doors in the rooms be closed properly nor did the loo have a full-fledged door. It was barely two feet tall! Why did they have to be frugal with the loo door? Well, that prompted the boys to take possession of a housing construction site adjacent to their motel. The site had several tiny rooms demarcated through half-constructed walls, barely three feet high, open to the sky. Each of the men earmarked their territory there for the morning ritual and even boasted the following day about their simultaneous and silent contemplation of the shapes of the clouds in the sky above. They are fortunate that they were not noticed, and hence not shooed away right in the midst of the confluence of evacuation and contemplation!

Mostly it was to do with the sighting of the tip of Mount Kailash once again, but partly due to Satpal's negotiating skills that the latter part of the day at Darchen turned out to be delightfully dramatic. In the evening, they decided to amble into the one and only busy street of Darchen. It was a place unlike any other. Old and young men, shabbily dressed, were seen playing games! Quite literally. They were immersed in a pool game oblivious to the world, the tourists, for that matter anyone walking past, with their pool table finding its pride of place on the roadside. Unlike the eve-teasers our four women had encountered on the first day of camping, here was a breed of men who didn't want to look up for fear they might lose their game! The marketplace either had furious shoppers, buying little showpieces they could decorate their homes with, or woollens before they embarked upon the *parikrama* of Mount Kailash.

Anita and Anurita ended up in a shop that sold jewellery made of colourful stones. They had not quite forgotten the brilliantly coloured stones at Manasarovar. Excitement took the better of them, and they collected a neat packet which they decided to buy for no more a solid reason than the fact the jewellery reminded them of their favourite lake, and had the compensating virtue of looking good on them. Fortunately for them, but rather unfortunately for the shopowner, Satpal happened to chance into the same shop.

**Satpal:** You are buying these huge rings and necklaces, Anita?

**Anita:** Yes, so is Anurita. Look at her collection.

**Anurita:** Aren't they beautiful?

**Satpal:** (in Hindi) Never praise the goods in a shop in the hearing range and the language of its owner. He will raise the price.

**Anita:** But this is not India. He might be telling us the right price and he is so friendly.

**Satpal:** No shopkeeper of any standing anywhere in the world can let an opportunity like you guys pass by. Let me handle this.

**Anurita:** What are you going to do?

**Satpal:** Tell me the total amount that he has asked from you, and just walk out of the shop.

**Anita and Anurita:** Yeah, but....

**Satpal:** Trust me.

Reluctantly, the two told him what he wanted to know and walked out of the shop, silently bidding an almost tearful farewell to the jewellery selected by them. After five minutes that seemed like five hours to them, Satpal silently emerged from the shop with nothing in his hands. Oh no, now the shopkeeper would never entertain the women again. They would miss their chosen jewellery all their lives. It was a bad start to the *parikrama*. They should not have allowed anyone to come in between them and their precious stones. All kinds of thoughts crossed their mind.

Satpal walked over gingerly to the ladies with a somewhat sheepish tell-all look to his face.

**Anita:** I knew that guy would not bargain. You shouldn't have sent us out.

**Anurita:** I really loved those stones. I want them.

**Satpal:** (Fishing out two packets from his deep trouser pockets) Here you are. I got them for you at 50 percent lesser than what he quoted.

**Anurita:** Really?

**Anita:** How did you do it?

**Anurita:** But you were hardly gone for five minutes!

Like butter on hot toast, word of Satpal's amazing talent spread within the group. He was grabbed by each of them one by one to help bargain for a cap, or a Tibetan fur coat, or incense sticks, or some more jewellery. Satpal willingly obliged and ran from one shop to the other that entire evening, with twinkling eyes and the satisfied smirk of a businessman who had just made some unexpected and huge profit. The thrill of bargaining till the last yuan seemed to have added life to his years!

On the way back from the marketplace, a voice hailed them; it proceeded from Kumaril, standing at the corner of the road with another group of about 10–11 Kailash-Mansaraovar *yatris*. These *yatris* stood out from the rest of the crowd due to their loud blue blazers with red striped sleeves.

**Kumaril:** These guys are returning from the trek!

Kumaril's announcement was the cue for much excitement and many anxious voices to take off together on a questioning spree.

**Kumaril:** Hold your horses. I have already gathered all the information. They could not complete the *parikrama*. They had to return yesterday from Dirapukh due to snowfall and heavy rains. And it is tough!

**Man from the other group:** And breathing gets increasingly difficult as you climb.

**Woman from the other group:** Do check the weather predictions before you leave.

**Another man from the other group:** And did you hear about the accident? This guy, who is a doctor himself, slipped and fell because of the melting snow, somewhere after Dirapukh. He has broken several bones, yet to be counted. It took 36 hours to get him out. That is why our group decided to return from Dirapukh itself.

This entire conversation sort of quietened our protagonists for a complete two minutes, until Supriya called out to them from a shop across the road, 'Come, have a look at the Tibetan woollens. They are so warm'. All thoughts of the incremental difficulties ahead were promptly relegated to an irretrievable corner of their memory space. And they forgot to check the weather!

Dinner was served that night in a room that was designated as the dining hall, but was no more than a stinking and greasy space surrounded by four walls and topped with a ceiling. You had to be careful while walking in the room, lest you slip on the oily floor. Probably the group was too hungry to notice it or the special treat laid down on tables covered in white table cloth was too inviting; either way, they slurped their meal down, in sheer enjoyment, all the way down their alimentary tract, with not a single thought or word spared for the putrid atmosphere.

It was only after the meal that it dawned on the women that they were fed as though for the last time before being consumed by nature. Once again multiple worries engulfed them; they were more than a tad fearful if not in awe of what awaited them the next day. The lack of oxygen was already being felt, and it was beginning to compound their apprehensions. Post dinner, their conversation comprised everything they thought they would encounter the next day, that is, on Day One of the *parikrama*. The feeling was like what is felt a night before the exam. Each one was prepared and yet, anxious about taking the 'test'. On their way back to their room, they tried to reason out with the experience of the other group of tourists they had met earlier that day.

**Anurita:** I don't think one must get bogged down by the experiences of another. I think reaching here is a blessing in itself.

**Satpal:** And these rooms are quite an experience unto themselves!

**Swati:** I look forward to whatever the future holds for me.

**Supriya:** Absolutely, be positive and move on.

**Anita:** *Parikrama,* here we come!

As I said earlier, none of the 14 were in the habit of worrying too long over a tomorrow, which was not even promised. In any case what could be tougher than the challenges of cycling uphill for hours at a stretch, or so they assumed!

Later in the night, the women of the Support Group stood outside their room to watch the night sky and began chatting about how they were closing in on what was going to be the signature of their lives, the eternal mountain.

**Anurita:** For all these years of being a journalist, I often came across people who would come and share their experiences of Manasarovar with me. Some came with invitations for a photography exhibition, others came with little books where they narrated their personal experience of the *parikrama* and what it meant to them. I particularly recall listening to one young girl, in her late twenties, about the difficulties she faced until she reached the base of Mount Kailash and how everything thereon, although tough, went smooth for her. Divine intervention, I offered, as she nodded in agreement. Another former colleague had long ago shared experiences of the Manasarovar *yatra* he undertook, the one organised by the Ministry of External Affairs. He said it was the one thing he wanted to do ever since he was a seven-year-old boy. Back then, as I was listening to him, I wondered if I would ever consider taking the *yatra*. Not because it was tough or the epitome for any Hindu to consider, but because I wasn't in the least the extreme adventure-loving sorts. For me, holidays meant either long walks alongside nature with stays in comfortable hotels or places buzzing with people including beaches and festival towns. My belief in God and how everything happens as per the Lord's will were unwavering though. But, I never quite thought I would be here—just a little away from Mount Kailash and that too with a group of cyclists. Indeed, this is such a miracle. I believe that everything is preordained.

**Anita:** Yes, dots connect, patterns fall in place.

**Supriya:** I can't help but agree. . .how else do I digest the fact that I am here. I hate to leave Jolly. I am sure he must be looking for me just as I have been remembering him all these days.

**Swati:** You bet! That I am here was fated too.

**Anurita:** And so was it fated that we would have to witness the theatrics of our drivers, and sleep in discomfort only to later recall these memories, both, fondly and funnily!

The awesome foursome shared some laughs and retired to their room. Once there, the strange smell emanating from the room made it uncomfortable for them to fan the desire to sleep. But they knew they had to fight everything to have a good night's sleep. After all, the following day would be a long, long one.

# 18

***INEFFABLE***

***In-effay-bl***

*(adj) Origin: Latin*

*Too great, powerful, or beautiful to be expressed in words*

**DAY ELEVEN:** *Darchen to Yam Dwar to Dirapukh*

Sleep didn't greet the women well the previous night. They were, to put it mildly, struggling to overcome the insalubrious room. It smelled like headache oil, mildew and sweaty feet. With the sole aim of distracting their olfactory senses they did attempt to amuse themselves, by gossiping about their mothers-in-law, even role playing some old-fashioned melodrama. But this hot, spicy and all-time favourite subject too failed to diffuse the situation. The next morning at 7 am, as they walked out of their room for breakfast, a more encouraging and relieved expression could not have been seen than the ones resting in their twinkling eyes. 'This is the last time we are staying in that room' was written large, conspicuous and euphoric on their faces.

After a quick breakfast followed by loading of duffle bags on the bus, it was time to move to Yam Dwar to begin the first day of the *parikrama* around Mount Kailash. Yam Dwar (*Yam* is the Hindu god of death, and *Dwar* means a gate) is at 4,730 metre and located at Tarboche. The belief is that to enter the holy abode of Lord Shiva, one must overcome the fear of death, by passing through the gateway of death. This gateway symbolises the act of leaving behind your mortal body along with its sins, before entering the Lord's house for attaining emancipation. Yam Dwar is a small temple-like structure built in the Buddhist tradition, where you walk in from a doorway, get into a narrow passageway and walk out the opposite doorway. It takes less than a minute to get over the fear of death!

Anita had already explained the legend behind this place in Mayumula to the girls. Savitri, a rare combination of a god-fearing and a husband-loving woman, was married to Satyavan. Sadly, he died young. *Yama* came to take Satyavan's soul away, but as he was returning, Savitri began to walk with him. They became friends and Yama felt obliged to grant her three boons as long as she did not ask for Satyavan's life. Genius that she was, Savitri first asked for her father-in-law to return to his kingdom from exile as the King; next she asked that the King may have more sons to compensate for his dead son, Satyavan, and lastly that Savitri herself may have a hundred sons. Yama granted all three boons and only then realised that the last boon required Satyavan to be alive. Lo and behold! Satyavan came alive right at this very spot, the *Yam Dwar*! Here is another intriguing piece of information. According to Indian scriptures, there are five forms of support that assist the Lord of Death, in hastening death—*Jwaar* (fever), *Vyadhi* (disease), *Krodha* (anger), *Asuya* (envy) or *Kaal* (time). And Satyavan was afflicted by which of these could be anybody's guess!

The group boarded the bus, each immersed in thoughtful silence, in the 10-minute ride to Yam Dwar. A few long sighs laced with marvel and appreciation were released on sighting Gurla Mandhata (7,649 metre) on the way. It is called Namo Nanyi or Fairy's Peak in local parlance and is revered by the Buddhists, in particular. First ascended in 1985, this is the 35th highest peak in the world, if that's of any interest to you.

On reaching Yam Dwar at about 9 am, they began their long and impatient wait for the porters, yaks and horses. As Shakespeare said, time is very slow for those who wait. Now here is the moment where you must comprehend that the porters in this region do not perceive the world in the manner we do. For them, time is a factor that does not even exist on any horizon, in any universe. You may term them laidback, but I think these are just the manifold ways of God, exposing us to the possibilities of nurturing calmness by slowing down our lives. The first of the porters began arriving a little after 10 am. By 11 am, three of the seven yaks booked by the group had marked their presence. The porters were females—young, sturdy and cherubic. The yak-keepers were men—tough and stocky. The rest of the porters, yaks and horses would certainly make it that day itself, the group was ceremoniously informed.

Amidst immense confusion about porters accompanying different groups (there were at least 20 other people waiting out there to begin the *yatra*), Harsh took the decision to leave Mauley and team behind to get the act of bags and porters together and catch up later, while the rest of the group members could begin the trek. And that is how 14 pairs of shapely limbs plunged into the 18 km-long *kora*. *Kora* is the Tibetan word for circumambulation done with the purpose of pilgrimage.

It was a misty day, with a few clouds playing truant and effectively hiding the peak of Kailash from plain view. When you begin the trek to Dirapukh, it is a level walk. The definition of a level walk in the mountains is any walk with the hidden motive of killing you or just short of it! One minute you are delighting in the comely beauty of the surroundings, and the next you are grappling with your elusive breath. But the group was in no hurry; they were stopping at every gradient, every curve, ever so often to breathe in the beauty and purity of the hills, the waterfalls, and the blue sky that enveloped them like a dome, almost like a mother would her child. The earthen track that appeared to go on endlessly for miles ahead to some unseen place, soon began to melt in the clouds.

At 11.30 am, the two horses, one for Kumaril and one for Anita, emerged from the landscape with their horsemen in tow, and caught up with the group. The horsemen belonged to two different generations, and collectively they had an average age of 45. Kumaril's horseman was bent over with age; countless wrinkles inhabited his face and hands. He could barely walk two steps without breathing hard. He was at least 70 years old, if not more. Anita's horseman was a pudding; young and spritely, tall and rugged, handsome and macho, dimpled and fair, you know the kinds young women drool about all over social media. He looked to be a strapping 21-year-old. If there is one thing Kumaril prides himself on, it is his gift of engaging in searching conversations, and the advent of his dated horseman provided the requisite provocation for him to pander in it right away.

**Kumaril:** It is only a matter of time.

**Anita:** For what?

**Kumaril:** My horse guy to collapse. He is tragedy.

**Anita:** Mine is an action-thriller!

**Kumaril:** (To the old man) Hey *Kaka*, can you walk the horse?

The old man gave a toothless smile and vigorously nodded his head.

**Kumaril:** Surely *Kaka*, this sort of thing cannot be good for your age.

**Old man:** What's wrong with my age? I am 25!

**Kumaril:** Then why don't you have teeth?

**Old man:** Even babies don't have teeth!

Kumaril's jaw had fallen several notches by this time.

**Anita:** Ha ha ha. Remind me to ask my horseman his age.

**Kumaril:** Please do so now. I am curious.

**Anita:** Hey, what's your name? (calling out to the young horseman)

**The young man:** Muwyma.

**Anita:** How old are you?

**Muwyma:** I don't know, probably same as him (pointing to Kumaril).

Anita was in fits. She was shaking with laughter, holding her stomach. Kumaril, meanwhile, had suddenly developed extreme respect for all horses and people attached to horses, more because he felt vindicated that he looked ever so young despite his burgeoning 40s, and less because of any equestrian inclinations.

**Kumaril:** I guess they have a system of telling their age. We must respect their system.

**Anita:** You are trending, Kumaril!

Anita and Kumaril's adventures with horse riding alongside a boy and a man getting on in years, began thus.

The group had been walking for an hour and were perhaps in the grip of an assured certainty that during the cycling expedition they had already seen the best weather, most outstanding sceneries, prettiest water bodies and physically most challenging routes. Sometimes we forget to remember that there is an unknown future eagerly awaiting us just around the corner, and it is more than likely that it holds fresh, new and even unfathomed challenges. The group had been amply warned that once they began the *parikrama*, they were not to expect any medical help in the entire route, and if the atmosphere offered any discomfort or even instant death to the oxygen starved, then the blame would land squarely on their own shoulders. But they were not worried, they had Harsh. Harsh, on the other hand, felt even more responsible for the group now.

An hour into the trek a short break was called for, one, to admire the tip of Mount Kailash that had just become visible by the clearing of the mist, and two, to mull on their fate-driven passport to paradise. When you stop in the mountains, whatever intervals your breath maybe repeating at, you sort of feel liberated into the environs. Even if it is cold outside, inside the mind, it is a warm, welcoming and an oddly otherworldly feel. The lap of Mount Kailash felt exactly like that. The air out there felt so clean that you dared not breathe out too hard into it and unnecessarily perturb it. At a distance, hidden somewhere in the eminence of the deep blue sky was their destination, yet just beholding the peak felt as if they had already arrived. It conveyed an energy so proximate, that they began to feel in coherence with the setting.

Harsh, Rajiv, Gaurav, Supriya, Atul and Anita waited for the others to catch up. Anurita and Kuldeep were taking it slow and steady, but the rest caught up soon enough. Break time was also food time. Each of them was either carrying chocolates or dry fruits. But Gaurav was carrying coffee-flavoured GU Gel, if you please! Anita was already feeling the first pangs of exhaustion creeping in. She grabbed one GU Gel from Gaurav's kitty and decided to forge ahead of the group. Atul went along. Anita is petite, her stride is small, and the path forward was neither gentle, nor easy. She had barely walked a few hundred feet, when Atul realising that her breathing was a little too noisy, cajoled her into doing a bit of the trek on horseback. The horse turned out to be a pony and more like an elephant in its gait. It kind of swung its hips needlessly from side to side like models do on a ramp walk. Though ponies and horses are the speediest way to complete this trek, you must have a fluid body that is used to jerks and swinging motions as a matter of habit, to be able to tolerate the ride. Anita sat rather obliquely on the horse and struggled to stay put. The world appeared lopsided and the horseman somewhat angular. Anita could not take it beyond a kilometre. But exactly when she decided it was enough, Muwyma was nowhere to be found. The horse was suddenly on its own, with no one to guarantee its intellect, experience or superiority in the management of a female, so frightened, that the peak of the divine mountain visible right overhead was also no consolation. Then, as suddenly as he had disappeared, Muwyma manifested himself from some rock...at least that's what Anita's theatrical mind would believe.

**Anita:** Muwyma, I want to get off.

**Muwyma** smiles, dimple and all. Says nothing.

**Anita:** Muwyma, my knees hurt. Can you stop your animal, please?

**Muwyma** smiles, dimple and all. Says nothing. Winks at her.

**Anita:** Muwyma! Do you understand? I am uncomfortable.

**Muwyma** smiles, dimple and all. Says nothing. Continues striding ahead, with the confidence of Mister Universe.

**Anita:** MUWYMA! HELP ME GET OFF THE HORSE NOW!

**Muwyma:** Yes. There. (Pointing to a rock a few metres away where it undoubtedly would be easier for her to get off).

Longish silence.

**Anita:** Muwyma.

**Muwyma** smiles, dimple and all. Says nothing.

**Anita:** Thank you.

**Muwyma** smiles, dimple and all. Says nothing.

Muwyma helped Anita off the animal and that was the last she heard or saw of him that day. Later, when she once again felt the need to take a little rest from trekking, the young horseman had become a source of wonder and mystery for Anita: she kept wondering how someone could have such an innocent smile on such a freakishly handsome face, and how he could magically disappear in the vast and open expanse, exactly when she needed to ride.

In the evening, when she exchanged notes with Kumaril on the equine experience, he had the same story to tell. His '25'-year-old, too, had vanished with the speed of a 21-year-old, without a thought for his 'youthful' client, who had paid in advance for the luxuries of a horse ride on a difficult trek. A piece of advice from a veteran set of two wheels: on the roads of Tibet, for adventure, for smelling-seeing-hearing-feeling nature or just to get a kick out of life, it is cycles that you must look for. But if any of you land up trekking here in these serene surroundings, then for obtaining excitement and thrill, all you need to do is hire horses/ponies, and then spend the rest of your trek searching for your horsemen (they-of-totally-unexcitable-and-unruffled-disposition) and their animal attachments.

Atul caught up with Anita almost as soon as she got off the horse. He was walking literally with horsepower! The others were not far behind. They were six kilometres into the trek. So far they had seen only the tip of Mount Kailash. They kept looking skywards, intermittently, in the hope of catching a glimpse again. The cloud covering the peak of the mountain initially did not display enough character to recede in order to give a clear view to my 14 friends. However, like breaking news, it abruptly shifted to reveal not just the tip but the torso of the southern flank too. The mountain rose unchallenged, its peak covered with snow. The shape of the mountain is unique. Yes, this was it, thought Anita. I am in God's presence, thought Anurita, who was not far behind. A bit of the mountain was beginning to take residence inside them.

At mid-point in the trek there were a host of straggly huts offering all the potato chips of the world to go along with hot tea served in squishy plastic cups. Satpal was already there sipping tea, looking dishevelled, and in consternation, when Atul and Anita reached there. He was unwell. Satpal's lungs, charged with compressed fatigue, were seeking revenge. His head was splitting with pain and he was nauseous. Lack of oxygen affects you like that. Anita was carrying a painkiller, because it was she who was an asthmatic, it was she who was expected to get a headache, it was she who was not supposed to be comfortable with the height. But she was absolutely fine; not even excessive shortness of breath now. Anita gave the painkiller to Satpal. As she turned around from the hut to look at the sky, she yelled in ecstatic delight. They were right below the Nagphani (the feature on the top of Kailash where the snow forms the shape of a cobra's hood) and the view was stunningly, enchantingly and radiantly clear. The goodwill, the charm and the enigma of the place continued to seep in further.

The rest of the trek was often steep, fairly rough, full of rocks and boulders, with slim waterfalls clinging to surrounding hills, and a smattering of deer, wild asses, drongos, crows, yaks, and stray dogs, but packed with poignant nature in a magically self-contained world. The latter half of the trek was picturesquely positioned alongside the Lha Chu River. It took them over five hours to reach Dirapukh, and that included two long and several tiny breaks. No sweat? Well, not really. Satpal and Kuldeep, two of the stronger ones of the group, were quite uncomfortable with only 52 percent oxygen available compared to that at sea level. Fatigue had gripped their lungs more than it did their muscles. It could happen to anybody.

Dirapukh is located in the valley of Lha Chu River. Chhuku Gompa looks down gently from a hill at Diraphuk, at rows of tin housing for about hundred *yatris* at a time. This is the highest elevation in the *parikrama* where trekkers spend a night; many are known to turn back from here after spending a restless night due to scarcity of oxygen. The accommodation of my 14 was situated right at the feet of Mount Kailash. The north face of the mountain is visible from here in full glory, and in fact, appears to be at touching distance. This is the best view that the mountain offers in the 52 km-long *parikrama*. The vision of the mountain so close and overhead is decidedly sublime. Fatigued muscles come to life here and the unyielding mind and thoughts become restful. A kind of magnetic pull is felt down to the very core; it brings out the love in you, the warmth in you, the worship and the ocean-like generosity that is trapped inside. It is as if all secrets of life lay bare before you; you must only rise from its ashes and glide into eternal bliss. You sense the seamlessness of nature: you become the mountain and the mountain becomes you. This surely was the place that nudges you to reach past the kingdom that is within the mind to find one's soul, to become much more; this was the place to die for. Immediately on reaching Dirapukh, Anita and Anurita watched the mountain in quiet stillness, absorbing its energy and feeling blessed, for as long as the call for hot soup did not reach their ears!

The Dirapukh stay was a surprise package. Cold but not cold enough, windy but not chilly enough, comfortable beds but not clean enough, and no water and no loo or loo tent. For the first time in their entire trip, the group was going to stay in tin sheds. The greatest allure of tin sheds is their sociability. You can hear your friends breathe or so much as stir in the next room; when it is windy you can feel the chill conveyed through the cracks in the windows while making repeated and successful attempts to freeze you; the reeking smell of the remnants of multiple and active digestive systems flows in unhindered from the outside; you can see the mess surrounding the place that you are inhabiting for one night, and yet because you are in Dirapukh, you can simply drown in the quietness of the place so lovingly nestled at the feet of Mount Kailash. 'Height' of mixed emotions, that's what it is.

**Anurita:** Amazing, isn't it, that we are touching the sacred mountain and are, in a way enveloped by it?

**Anita:** Can't seem to take my eyes off or remove my body either.

**Anurita:** Can you see the forms on Mount Kailash like I can?

**Anita:** If you look closely, the facade appears to be in the form of the face of Lord Shiva, with a Ganesha-like form on the east flank and a Parvati-like form on the west flank of the mountain. Or am I hallucinating!

**Anurita:** No, you are not, I see them too. I feel lucky to be right here, touching Mount Kailash and being blessed by the Lord for making it happen.

In the evening, the group collected in the boys' room. Hot noodle soup was served followed by *khichdi*. They sailed into the rice and pulses, and raised hell with the war on cholesterol by defiantly adding dollops of butter. No tedious questions were raised at the shortage of water and oxygen among other things. Life was good. Later, a few hospitable heads of the tin-shed management peered in through the door one by one, evidently to check the level of enjoyment of the food by the guests, but mostly to regard their own efforts at providing such a 'comfort-ridden' place to foreigners.

Anurita, Kuldeep, Satpal, Anand and Supriya took the decision to go back to Darchen the next day. They were drained beyond measure: Satpal had to take oxygen to get back his breath; Kuldeep, otherwise raring to go and energetic, was uncomfortable with the way his health was treating him after the long, winding walk. Or perhaps it was the dip in Lake Manasarovar where he caught a cold which aggravated within. No point in trying to test limits when the body decides to unfriend you temporarily, they collectively thought. I have no position on trekkers and trekking, but it would be inconsiderate on my part to disagree with them.

The sun had set, darkness had fallen and the women could no longer battle with their bladders. A quiet place, away from the din of the kitchen and the tents of the porters, had to be found. They ambled around in a charmingly indecisive manner until they found a spot. Activity completed, out of sheer force of habit they looked upwards, and were rewarded with a spectacular night sky, never seen before by the 10 pairs of eyes. The sky was studded with stars, constellations and a half moon. The mountain was glowing like a bride in the confident light cast by the moon and starlight; the effect was hypnotic. Three of the girls, wearing fewer layers and therefore freezing more per cubic inch, soon left for the cosy comfort of their creaky beds, but Anita and Anurita stayed on. They stood there for a long time, reverentially gazing at the divinity before them. If the sky was the limit, why did it feel like there were no limits here, they wondered.

The night's sleep was quiet and peaceful.

# 19

***UBUNTU***

***oo-boon-too***

*(noun) Origin: South African*

*The belief in a universal bond of sharing that connects all humanity*

**DAY TWELVE:** *Dirapukh to Zutulpukh via Dolma La*

The trek to Zutulpukh Gompa was all of 22 km and when Atul, who had done this once before, informed the group of its difficulties and challenges, everyone recognised the truth in the man's words. Although it does seem very tough when you read about it, but it was tougher in reality. It was a trek that could make even concrete limbs to buckle when you need them the most. A height gain of almost 2,000 feet (16,800 feet at Dirapukh to 18,600 at Dolma La Pass) plays havoc with the body.

Medical science identifies three categories of mountain altitudes in terms of its effects on the human body: High altitude (4,500–11,500 feet), Very high altitude (11,500–18,000 feet) and Extreme altitude (above 18,000 feet); each of these altitudes require immense adaptation by the human body. Tibet itself, with an average elevation of 14,800 feet, comes in the very high-altitude category. Inhabitants of Tibet are acclimatised to scarce oxygen, however, for outsiders, the body takes a while to adapt. Most people who come here to trek, experience some or the other form of Acute Mountain Sickness (AMS), headache, nausea, etc., or sometimes exhaustion to the point of no return. You have seen earlier how Satpal had hit a wall, and Kuldeep was close to it. They made a wise decision to return. The best treatment for AMS is to lose height, or climb down. At extreme altitude, the ultimate risk is that of brain damage, therefore, humans plan not to stay there too long. Above 26,000 feet is considered as the 'Death Zone' where it is impossible for the human body to acclimatise. With the slow loss of vital functions, and confused mental state in this region, mountaineers climbing mountains such as Everest are advised to 'touch and go'. The next day of the trek/climb was, therefore, going to be extraordinary.

They started at sharp 7 am that day; nine of the group members proceeded to Zutulpukh, while five started back for Darchen. Since the Darchen trek is fresh in your minds, I will focus here on the trek to Zutulpukh for now. The scenic route had a familiarity about it, but the trail was as new as it gets.

There is an old Tibetan saying:

*If you don't carry him up the hill,*
*You are no pony;*
*If you cannot walk down the hill,*
*You are no man.*

Of all the things you long for in a mountainous setting, a walk down the hill is first in preference and a genuine 'level walk' is perhaps the next most desired. The trek that day began with a steep climb uphill. The body and mind were put to test with a preamble that gave no inkling of things to come, but the group had fortified their minds to complete it. Even then, it was an unequal match all along, between mountain and man!

Atul climbed considerably better than the others; it was kind of expected from a swashbuckling Everester! The strongest in the group though, Gaurav, Harsh and Haresh were somewhat stunned by the continuous climb towards lesser and lesser life-giving oxygen, but were not going to be quelled by it. Swati and Sanjeeta had fallen behind. Kumaril was keeping track of his horseman, and Rajiv was finding it increasingly difficult to appreciate his own decision to undertake this trek. The constant endeavour of the trekkers was to plunge into the mountain, climb 100–200 metres, emerge huffing and puffing, stop for a few seconds, admire the picturesque setting, thank the heavens for good weather, and then repeat.

Anita tried to negotiate the climb for a while, but her lungs were rather obstinate that day. Mercifully, Atul had insisted that Muwyma walk right beside him. He suggested that Anita ride the few kilometres uphill towards Dolma La Pass. She was initially hesitant, but better counsel prevailed when she realised that her respiratory system was threatening to dispense with its services to her body. On horseback, she climbed uphill in a jiffy. The north-east face of Kailash, rugged and rocky, could be seen all along. It pulsated with an irresistible energy. The air had become rarer, but she was just fine.

A kilometre short of Dolma Pass, having covered close to 4 km, Anita dismounted. Despite the winter chill she had beads of perspiration on her forehead due to the incessant and throbbing pain in her knees. She no longer could take it. Yes, oftentimes it is much more painful for the knees on horseback as compared to walking. There was a continuous uphill climb from here and the Pass was not in sight. Anita began her slow, arduous yet mesmeric climb.

Announcing the proximity of the Pass, you come upon a place with thousands of prayer flags tied to tall poles. This is known as Shiva Tsal. Anita was amazed to find innumerable stone cairns draped with some discarded clothing or the other, a shirt, a scarf, a pair of jeans, even socks! She had read about this. After having overcome the fear of death at Yam Dwar, it is at this point in the *parikrama,* where it is believed the pilgrims undergo symbolic death. On crossing the Dolma La they are reborn and thus begins yet another cycle of birth and death. Tibetans leave some of their worn clothes, a lock of hair, a piece of jewellery or some drops of blood at this place, to indicate their entry into the new cycle of birth by leaving behind their past life at Shiva Tsal. Anita wished she had planned this beforehand and carried some extra clothes. The temperature was too low to even consider removing a sock, cap or muffler for this gesture. She looked up at the sky and begged forgiveness from the universe. Simultaneously, she requested for rebirth after crossing Dolma La, with a clear break from the past, all sins forgiven, including her deliberately forgetting to wish happy birthday to certain acquired relatives!

I need to speak about prayer flags here to ease you into a sublime mood. The hanging of prayer flags is a Bon tradition. At all high passes, on top of *stupas, gompas,* mountains, rooftops, temples and even on cairns you will find colourful prayer flags fluttering in the wind, conveying the prayers of humanity to the gods, as the Tibetans believe. A prayer flag will have a set of five flags placed next to each other in a specific order of colours representing the five elements—first the blue symbolising the sky, space and cosmos; then the white denoting the air and the wind; next the red associated with fire; the green signifying water and lastly the yellow embodying Mother Earth. Heights are chosen for prayer flags, because it is believed that they must never be still. And most fascinatingly, it is considered auspicious if the colours of the flags are faded; it means that your prayers have been carried by the winds to the person/ place they were meant for.

Often the flags carry the mantra, *Om Mani Padme Hum*. The 14th Dalai Lama explains its meaning as follows: 'The six syllables, *Om Mani Padme Hum*, mean that in dependence on the practice of a path which is an indivisible union of method and wisdom, you can transform your impure body, speech, and mind into the pure exalted body, speech, and mind of a Buddha.' You can carry your own mantra-ridden flags to Shiva Tsal, write your prayers on them, and tie them high up on the poles here, to begin their journey of flapping and transmission to the gods. Anita, of course, had forgotten to do so; her face registering a beseeching look, she addressed the flags and prayed with amazing clarity and swiftness, for blessings for her loved ones. It was cold and windy; she had to speed up.

There were hardly people that day; a handful of locals and a couple of Europeans. For the first 15 odd minutes or so, Anita transported to her own world, tranquil and joyous. Her legs were doing all the walking, her lungs the breathing, and her mind just connected to the mysterious energy and undisturbed beauty of the surroundings; now that is my idea of a perfect division of labour! But then that perfection lasted only 15 minutes! Muwyma, meanwhile, had taken the opportunity to disappear. Once again.

Just before the Pass, there is a precipitous climb leading up to it, full of moraine, stones and boulders, the smallest being the size of a football. You have to weave your way up the treacherous path very carefully. Right there, a Tibetan woman seasoned by time and years, overtook Anita in short but quick steps. The old woman smiled one of the most toothless smiles possible for a human adult and called out in the gentlest of manners to Anita, '*Ta-she-de-lehk*'. Though she was climbing at remarkable pace, she seemed neither tired nor anxious to reach the destination; there was something so peaceful about her. Anita, on the other hand, was no longer walking, she was stumbling; her energies had deserted her, her mind was like a record player gone bad, her eyes kept closing on her with grogginess and exhaustion, her limbs had gone AWOL, and the seeds of bewilderment at what exactly she was doing in these surreal surroundings were taking root. Another 15 minutes and she was struggling to recall if there was a destination, if at all there was an end. The last time she had experienced this kind of extreme fatigue and enervation was probably at childbirth. There was no telling when she would just collapse like a pack of cards. She was shaken to the core, beyond measure, beyond disbelief. If she had to get out of this place sane, in one piece and alive, she would have to allow her mind to take over the body, and pray for some semblance of intrepidness. She engaged herself in a meaningless conversation with herself.

**Anita 1:** This path that you have foisted on me, has jeopardised the chances of my returning to my kids.

**Anita 2:** But you are going to get a medal, for not initiating hostilities against your brain that urged you to go.

**Anita 1:** You listen to me, idiot! Get out of this place, if you know what is good for you.

**Anita 2:** What is good Phaedrus, and what is not? Who are we to decide such mundane things?

**Anita 1:** Why bring Phaedrus into this?

**Anita 2:** The guiding spirit of Plato. Or was it Aristotle? I am a little confused. I could do with some help here.

**Anita 1:** Let's kidnap both Plato and Aristotle, tie them up, torment them and force them to reveal who said what, and why did they have to make things so complicated.

And so it went on, until just before the Pass, when she, rather her body, was ready to give up, but not her mind. Something within told Anita that although there was not even a sporting chance of her body continuing any further, she was going to make it. She stood there, breathing hard and rapid, looking up towards the path that led up to the Pass, asking for strength from the universe. Perhaps, the all-encompassing consciousness that she so much believed in, would hear and help.

That is when she felt someone pushing her up. She turned around to see the pleasantly flushed face of a young female porter. Anita looked apologetic vis-à-vis the porter, who had not even an electron of a suggestion on her face that she was doing this out of sympathy or even concern. She was rather tall in comparison to the economy-sized Anita and had that indulgent look of a friend who was accustomed to throwing surprise parties for you each year. While not a single word was exchanged, Anita's eyes spelt gratefulness and then she unabashedly took her support and resumed the climb. The pushing must have helped, for she reached the Dolma La Pass. The female porter vanished as quickly as she had appeared. Anita felt a sense of relief, and life began to limp back to normal inside her; she yelled a loud 'thank you' directed at the universe but meant for the female porter at the Dolma La Pass, in the hope that the thin air would carry it to her. She got a grip on her situation—both mental and physical—and was happy to note that she had reached the Pass utterly dazed but unscathed. It was 11 am.

The Dolma La Pass is the highest point of the *parikrama* at 19,500 feet. 'Dolma' is the Tibetan name for Goddess Parvati, the consort of Lord Shiva. Hindus believe that this Pass is her residence. On descending to the other side of the Pass, right at the bottom, you can see the glacial waters forming an enchanting emerald green reservoir known as Gauri Kund. It is the bathing tub of the Goddess. The Buddhists believe that all three qualities of the Buddha—the mind, speech and the body—are alive in every rock, every stone found at the Dolma La (*La* means a pass).

It was subzero on the Pass. But who would be foolish enough to reach Dolma La and not pray for a while? A woman given to kinder impulses perhaps, but not Anita! The prayer lasted a full 30 seconds, before the illusion of her own toughness betrayed her once again, and inspiration, if any, failed her. Anita could feel the chill seep in through her tough trekking boots. Her feet soon became numb; chilblains were taking root; she could scarcely feel her face; the very fibres of her being were below freezing point. And then she was found descending from the Pass as swiftly as she was found praying. It was steep downhill. On one side of the narrow path was the mountain that formed the Pass, and on the other side a sheer fall into Gauri Kund. But suddenly, and for no discernible logic or reasoning, Anita had acquired wings. Was she actually reborn? Did the crossing of Dolma La affect one this way? She almost ran down the Pass, stopping only when a Tibetan trekker doing anti-clockwise *parikrama* required the right of way or when the trekker in front of her would stop for whatever purpose: breathing, photographing, admiring the view, encountering the mind, or simply revelling in the beauty of it all. On a track as slender as this, only at the peril of one's life and enthusiasm, one may try to overtake a fellow trekker.

The precarious downhill path lasted a good kilometre or so, and after crossing over some snow, she ended up in a terrain that was muddy and flat like a plain as far as the eyes could see. Was that it? Is the trek over? It took just three hours! Unbelievable that she had done it! But the sprightly rays of light on her triumphant horizon took a nosedive within minutes, for Atul caught up and informed that they had covered only six of the 22 km so far, and this was the valley leading to Dolma village! For eons Anita's fallen jaw and shocked eyes did not resume normalcy.

**Atul:** Are you having a fit or what? Put the jaw back to where it belongs, and start walking.

**Anita:** This is why Anita 1 has been admonishing me to lay off this trek.

**Atul:** What are you talking about?

**Anita:** I am not really reachable right now, you know!

Now Atul knew better than to persist. When Anita is tired and/or hungry, you do not aggravate her in any way, repeat DO NOT! He simply started to walk ahead, and Anita, like the lost lamb of Little Bo-Peep, just hung her head down and followed him listlessly. Finally, after another 1,000 odd metres, two welcome things happened. One, Muwyma surfaced from the soil, and two, they descended gently to another plain area, the Dolma village, conspicuous due to a tea shop and the confluence of two rivers—the Lha Chu and the Topchen Chu. These rivers arise from the Indus and meet at this spot to form the river Zhong Chu. The Zhong Chu gave company thenceforth to trekkers all the way to Zutulpukh.

Eyes lit with anticipation and making some idiotic noises about hunger pangs, Anita walked straight into the tea shop with Atul. The only blemish in what could have been the ultimate moment of unadulterated joy was the overpowering smell of butter, oil and yak cheese in the shop. Two men were bustling inside, serving soup and Tibetan tea to the customers. Anita and Atul were ushered straight to one of the seating areas that was so decrepit that they hesitated, but only for a moment. They ordered hot noodle soup and waited like impatient children waiting for their lollipops. There is this strange sounding laugh that resembles the whistle of a coal-based railway engine, which reflects the unplugged state of mind of a person. Anita employed it the moment the soup arrived. The laugh proceeded to infect Atul and the general atmosphere of the couch where they were seated was nothing short of merriment. Slurp! Slurp! Slurp! Hot noodle soup over in less than a minute! This was the life, and this was the moment!

The rest of the men from the group joined them just as the second round of soup was being ingested. Rajiv looked so dishevelled that he garnered sympathetic looks from all, including Anita. Swati and Sanjeeta had fallen behind by now and though Harsh felt reassured that they were together, concern was writ large on his face for the two of them. It was time to move. Anita cannot walk fast even if you let loose a grizzly bear behind her. She cannot talk loud, even if she is required to yell to save her life. But she is a person who prides herself on her unpredictability. She never knows when she might start running, when she may just collapse only to be carried on a stretcher, or when she may find or lose her voice. Atul knew this a bit too well. He goaded her into starting the journey of the next 15 km on horseback, without waiting for the others to catch up. Smiling, dimpled Muwyma helped her up the pony/horse. Anita began the longest, loneliest trek of her life in the company of one horseman, three yaks-men, two female porters named Meh and Yalmin, four yaks and of course, the horse, none of whom could communicate much in any language on earth known to her, not even baby tongue.

It so happened that once again, Anita's knees could not bear the excruciating pain of the ride, hence after 3 km, she got off the horse. The terrain hereon is not exactly a level walk, but extremely winding, undulating and as unending as the cosmos itself. The rest in the group were yet to catch up, and she had 11 km more to cover. She had the choice of either waiting for them or attempting to walk, nay run, at their pace, or go ahead with these people and animals. She chose the latter.

And thus began the walk alongside river Zhong Chu with the incommunicados.

What was notable about this arrangement was that the yaks were impish (being of high spirit and boundless energy, they are given to suddenly go off the track, or just walk straight into you, horns and all, if you are careless enough) and the burly yaks-men often pointed at Anita, uttered some gibberish and laughed loudly. But she was unfazed, for she had been won over by the elegantly gentle concern of Meh and Yalmin over her continuous breathlessness, expressed by taking turns to rub her back at intervals. It strangely made her feel better. A nice but unsentimental one-time friendship was in the offing. There is this natural bonhomie amongst women whenever and wherever they meet. Anita says that even the protons of a mother can recognise the protons of another mother. There is something about motherhood that transforms women to become sensitive about each other's needs. It bonds them across all frontiers and artificial boundaries. All three women in this case had been able to somehow get across to each other that they had two daughters each!

Though different and spectacular facets of Mount Kailash were visible for a fairly large part of this trek, the mountain had completely disappeared from sight at around 2 pm. Anita had earlier used the vision of the sacred mountain rising right before her eyes to negotiate the trek, but now it was just her, her incommunicable friends, the river, the sound of the breeze whooshing past, the chiming of yak bells, and the track.

When a challenging destination masquerades in the guise of excitement, one may keep trying to convince the muscles, but after a point they refuse to even give it a fair consideration. Anita was beginning to feel groggy once more. Conscious of the rapid approach of exhaustion, she used her remaining energy to focus on breathing. Breathe in, take one step, breathe out, and take another step. She knew it wasn't too long before the tempests of fatigue would get lowered and all this would be well behind her, in the past, and she wouldn't even be able to recall these tumultuous moments with clarity. In the midst of this agitation of spirit, I have to narrate a Zen *Koan,* here and now:

> A student went to his meditation teacher and said, 'My meditation is horrible! I feel so distracted, or my legs ache, or I'm constantly falling asleep. It's just horrible!'
>
> 'It will pass,' the teacher said matter-of-factly.
>
> A week later, the student came back to his teacher. 'My meditation is wonderful! I feel so aware, so peaceful, and so alive! It's just wonderful!'
>
> 'It will pass,' the teacher replied matter-of-factly.

Anita continued to limp, lurch, strut, slog and scramble. She would look quizzically at Muwyma ever so often, and ask in weak gestures how much further Zutulpukh was. He would smile the dimpled smile of a man who knows that now is the time to come to the aid of a damsel in distress, but sadly did not know how to go about it. Accompanying that smile, would be an arm pointed in any general direction, and his mouth would form the words, 'It is there.' Each time she would surmise that there must be some indeterminate distance left, and Muwyma would purposely not reveal it just yet to avoid any death in custody. His custody.

It was 3.55 pm by Anita's watch. Her throat was as though permanently parched, light seemed to be fading from her eyes, legs not responding much to brain signals, and all she could think of was, why did the Chinese have to make them walk so much on the second day of the *parikrama*? After all, it was only a matter of erecting some hopeless tin sheds and digging worthless loo holes at comfortable distances! She could take the walk no longer. In deep anguish she indicated to Muwyma that she wanted to do the rest of the trek to 'it-is-there' on horseback. Mr Dimples clicked his tongue as if saying no. That communication made Anita so distraught that she caught hold of the reins of the horse herself to make it stop and mount it.

Muwyma got the point, but his smile by now was stretching from ear lobe to ear lobe; he was, in fact, giggling! The yaksmen too seemed to be sharing a joke at her expense. They continued to snigger while Muwyma helped Anita on to the horse. Ignoring the jabs, she heaved a sigh of relief; but before the sigh could be fully released, the horse turned around a sharp bend and Muwyma gleefully pointed his arm in some direction. He once again declared, 'It is there.' To Anita's chagrin, 'it' was actually 'there' this time—the Zutulpukh Gompa up on a hill. Right below it, barely 50 metres away, were the much-needed and desired-almost-to-the-point-of-love, tin sheds. It was 4 pm. Anita had completed the second day of the gruelling trek, but not without becoming the source of comic amusement to her companions. She knew that the story of the woman who for the life of her did not understand the paths in the mountains or the machinations of horses, would be told and retold to their grandchildren and great-grandchildren, and it only made her proud that she would be honoured thus in this strange and beautiful land.

The boys reached half an hour later. Atul was his usual energetic self and was just as alright as the tough Tibetans accompanying them, while Harsh and Gaurav showed signs of recovering from exhaustion, almost immediately on arrival. Kumaril and Haresh had paced out the trek in a doable manner, and hence fatigue was overcome with the help of just one bowl each of noodle soup. Rajiv, on the other hand, was unreachable for even his own mind, body and spirits, and collapsed on the bed of the rest house for at least a couple of hours after the day's trek. When he woke up, he looked thoroughly jangled, but curiously at peace.

Sanjeeta and Swati reached Zutulpukh at 7 pm after about 12 hours of gruelling trekking. It was dark by then, but the entire group felt very proud of them. What effort and what spirit! Though they had started the day with élan, the trek had often felt like an ordeal, less for its toughness, more for its never-endingness. Like the light slowly fading out of a battery-operated lamp, the duo did feel their body getting sapped of vital force, but it did not deter them the least bit. It is never pleasant for women regarded as strong and athletic, to find themselves in a situation where they are left behind by their group. However, on their part it was deliberate. Right from the beginning, Sanjeeta had requested Swati to be her trek partner and to maintain an even pace, which they did. What tipped the scales in their favour were the weather, and two Tibetan women porters who stayed with them all through. Swati and Sanjeeta found inspiration from something as inconsequential as the attire of the female porters, mainly their high-heeled shoes. If they could stride in those shoes with utmost ease, almost carelessly, then there was no doubt in their firm minds, that so could they in the comfort of their sports shoes. Finally, when they did reach Zutulphuk, the group needed no further evidence of their sheer tenacity and determination.

Therefore, the heroes for the day were Swati and Sanjeeta for their contemplations on high-heels among other things;

Rajiv whose strength went hither and thither and yet he pushed himself; Kumaril for trying his best to forge a curious relationship with a *Kaka* of indeterminate age; and Anita who was never expected to go beyond Diraphuk. Though, mind you, the rest had trekked all the way, unlike Anita who had done close to 7 of the 22 km on horseback.

At 7.30 pm when they sat together for hot soup, some might have been on the verge of becoming deliriously incoherent due to fatigue, but here at Zutulpukh they felt as if a lifelong passion for the outdoors laced with in-depth absorption of magnificence had been satisfied. Somehow, even though the focus of the group members on this trek was on the vastness and brilliance of nature and not on spirituality, they seemed to have imbibed the connection between humans and everything else around. The recognition that on the 4.5 billion-year-old Earth, their 70-odd years (God willing) were but a flash of awareness and experience, here now, gone forever, was deeply entrenched and entwined with a feeling of a fulfilled life. Even Mount Kailash had lived on Earth longer than several of their generations put together. They were humbled by it all.

After downing a bowl of noodle soup, Kumaril narrated the rollicking story of his flaming hope of riding a horse on this track and how it was dashed. It seems that to keep his horseman from doing the disappearing act on him, Kumaril literally walked hand-in-hand with the old man. The ancient one was genuinely out of gear, he would get very breathless and had to necessarily take rest after every 20 steps or so. Now Kumaril was not unnaturally anxious to ride, but he wasn't one to let go of any service he had paid for either. Though capable of walking the entire length of the trek, he had rented a horse due to the fever that had affected him since the first day of cycling. His curiosity at the capacity of the old man to handle a rider got the better of him after having covered several kilometres on foot. He told the '*Kaka*' that he wanted to do some riding. The toothless *Kaka* was happy to help; he stopped the horse and offered his bony thin arm as wavering support for Kumaril to climb on to the horse. Kumaril stepped on the support without hesitation, only to find himself launched reversely in the direction of the ground along with *Kaka*! That was the end of Kumaril's mushrooming relationship with the horse and the horseman!

That night, dinner was a relaxed affair. Kumaril was in his elements, all bounce, chirpiness and anecdotal and had one too many rib-tickling tales to tell. They chatted and laughed and constantly felt the permeation within of a soothing feeling of being blessed. The mountain's beauty and its challenges were a brilliant contradiction that they had come to respect. Their follies, their faults, their opinions, their judgments, their fortune and misfortune, had sunk into comparative insignificance beside the enormity of the mountain.

On the other side were the famous five who were trekking to Darchen. The trek from the previous day had given them a fair idea of all that lay ahead as they started out after a round of All the Bests and Good Lucks to their energetic nine. It was going to be a tough day. For one, while Satpal was quite unwell, and Kuldeep suffered from a congested nose, trekking for a day to reach back to Darchen was nothing short of an act of bravery, because you are literally 'driving on the wrong side'.

If you fall sick, develop high temperature, have frozen limbs or sharp aching bodies in urban settings, in the comforts of your home, you have the luxury to stay in bed and occasionally rise for healthy liquids that fuel your system, that spring you back to normalcy. But, none of that were to happen here. Despite not feeling well, Satpal knew he had to complete the day-long trek; Kuldeep was aware the winds were not going to be easy on his respiratory system. Both were a trifle reassured though, since they would get to gather their breaths and senses on reaching Darchen, and chiefly because they had the company of Anurita, Anand and Supriya.

However, it seems the powers of the universe infuse that extra bit of resolve even in the most trying circumstances and that is what happened with them.

Supriya, Anurita and Anand trekked along, soaking in the breathtaking beauty of the surroundings, this time lighter than they had felt the previous day. They couldn't believe it was the same trek they had taken the day before. It looked so beautiful and heavenly. Little red flowers by the gushing river, rocks and pebbles arranged by nature as though a piece of distinct art, the landscape along allowing them a peep into their childhood fairy-tale books; everything about the trek back to Darchen suddenly looked amazing. While the health of a couple of them was pale, there was no stress of 'completing' a certain number of kilometres to reach a designated spot. They spotted many people going up, many others coming down. Some greeted with smiles, some asked questions, and a few others preferred to stay quiet, nursing their meditative streaks. Anurita, perhaps, used her camera to the maximum that day. She also playfully ran her hands through little streams that promised to kiss some part of Mount Kailash for her. It was almost as though a part of her was dissipated and left behind in the vast magical landscape every time she stopped to walk through a stream, touch a beautiful flower, glance around the rich natural expanse or simply pose for a few photographs besides capturing many.

**Supriya:** The energy of this place is like that of a live electric wire, isn't it?

**Anurita:** Indeed. You know what, Supriya? The call of the mountain is a supreme one. Nothing that is beneath, around or scattered, can promise a similar energy, that is high, and more importantly, above all else. If one wishes to experience true-blue adventure, one needs to just get lost in the mountains!

**Supriya:** And nothing like mountains to make you believe that you can do it.

**Anurita:** Yes. In fact, all the more in the case of mountain climbing! Until held in the eyes and carefully wrapped with conviction, mountain-climbing is only a mirage.

**Supriya:** We got so involved in our talk that we forgot to even ascertain if everyone's feeling alright and can walk. Mountains teach you to forget and forgive too!

There were instances during the trek when the five wondered if they could have managed the trek up to Zutulpukh, when this one wasn't exactly a bed of roses. But, some of them, if not all, reasoned the 'whatever happens, happens for the good' mantra. And that's how it is too. There is a time and place for everything. Kuldeep believed he was lucky to have even made it to this trip considering he was the last to join in with the group, only after an important official conference he had to attend, fell through.

**Anurita:** This trip was never planned, it just happened for us. There was a larger 'will'.

**Supriya:** We had to be here, this time, this place, together.

*Gauri Kund seen from Dolma La, which is right above it*

*Photo credit: Atul Karwal*

*Raring to go but daring to take a break during the trek from Zutulphuk to Darchen*

*Photo credit: Atul Karwal*

**Anand:** And luck and destiny apart, I am glad each of us first willed it ourselves.

**Satpal:** Once we return, even these 'aching' moments will be memorable!

**Kuldeep:** For now, let's reach Darchen. On a lighter note, since we are but minute specks in the vast campus of this enormous nature, our aches and pains must be tinier still, and therefore insignificant! *Jai ho*!

# 20

***SERENDIPITY***

***Se-rendi-pitee***

*(noun) Origin: From a Persian fairy tale*

*The chance occurrence of events in a beneficial way; or luck that takes the form of finding valuable things that were not being looked for to begin with*

**DAY THIRTEEN:** *Zutulpukh to Darchen to Nyalam*

I have been bursting at my tyres (seams for you) to present the following Zen *Koan*, ever since I began this narration.

A master approached a young student who was in the process of locking his bicycle to the temple gate.

'Why are you locking your bicycle to the temple gate?' asked the master.

'Because I don't want it to get stolen,' replied the student.

'Who is it that you do not trust? Is it I?' asked the master.

'Surely not,' replied the student.

'Is it Yona, over there?' asked the master, pointing to another student on the other side of the temple.

'Surely not Yona,' replied the student. 'I do not know who it is that I do not trust.'

'In that case,' concluded the master, 'there is no reason in locking up your bicycle.'

The student followed the master's advice, and left his bicycle unlocked.

At the end of the day, when he returned to the temple gate, he discovered that it had been stolen.

'Master!' he cried, and the master came to his call.

'Master! I did as you advised, leaving the bicycle unlocked, because I did not know who it was that I do not trust, and look now. It has been stolen!'

'Ah,' replied the master. 'Then it is your own judgment that you did not trust. Your mind is changed too easily, son.'

And the student was enlightened.

The nine group members were determined to complete the *parikrama*. In their own judgment, particularly in the case of Anita, Swati and Sanjeeta, they were up to it, had tremendous faith in themselves and the grace of the cosmic consciousness. Their faith had not belied them, the grace from above never left them; they had, in fact, surrendered themselves to the mountain and completed the most difficult portion of the *parikrama*, eagerly awaiting the next and last leg. If faith can move mountains, judgment can help cross them!

On the last day of the trek, the group began their preparations to leave at 6 am. The three women went in three different directions for their ablutions. Anita decided to try out the 'hole' because she felt that this one was different—not in terms of the degree and spread of stench, but because the heap below seemed much farther down from the hole in the ground, thereby capable of preventing any contact between the mosquitoes swarming over the refuse and her skin. That was a luxury in these parts! Swati went right behind the wall that surrounded the 'hole' and Sanjeeta went into some bushes. By now, they were well adapted to the harsh living conditions of this area and were no longer losing their head, sleep or gossip over it. A bread-and-omelette breakfast was shoved in, as a leisurely ingestion just had to wait for the trek to get over.

The girls decided to have a quick look at the Zutulpukh or Zongzerbu Gompa, though only from a distance. They were done with all the climbing, at least for their immediate life and times. The Gompa is supposed to contain Milarepa's meditation cave and imprints of his feet and hands. They gazed at it from the bottom of the hill, and felt good, as if they had become worthy of nature. In its serenity, the Gompa seemed to announce that the journey of the mind, body and spirit that the group had undertaken in these parts may soon come to an end, but the three had affected each other to such an extent that if they dug deep they would find that the ethereal lake and the eternal mountain had taken root and were flourishing like a prayer within.

Led by Harsh, the rest of the nine began their last leg of the *parikrama* that day, leading back to Darchen, at 7.30 am. Once again Atul insisted that Anita do a small portion of the 12 km trek on horseback. Smiling, dimpled, handsome Muwyma, who was yet to get over his giggling fits from the previous day, and with whom Anita had parted on distant terms, helped her on to the saddle, specially designed for women to obtain an angular view of life. The boys went ahead, Anita followed, and Swati and Sanjeeta were a little behind at their own steady and happy pace.

Yet again, after a kilometre or two, the protesting knees brought Anita off the horseback. She joined the men in the walk. The track that day was gentle on the lungs, quadriceps, calf, hamstring and adductor muscles, if you know what I mean. It would wind upwards, now and then, but ever so gradually, that they hardly felt the scarcity of breath. Having climbed down from Dirapukh to Zutulpukh, their lungs were already adjusting to the atmosphere. Even if you are not enamoured with the outdoors, this is a place that can arrest your interest and warmth. The path that goes along River Zhong Chu is strewn with wild flowers in stunning colours. The river gushes over boulders right below, and the sound is that of a delightful shush in the silence!

Back in Darchen, the five group members who collectively decided to return on the second day of *parikrama,* owing to ill health (in case of Satpal and Kuldeep), safety and precaution (in case of Anand), absence of fierce drive to complete the *parikrama* (in case of Supriya) or generally as a design by the Force above (in case of Anurita who wanted to be with Kuldeep in this state of ill health he usually isn't prone to), the group was looking forward to tales of adventure and victory from the nine who managed the entire feat. Supriya and Anurita stepped out of their room after what was one of the most difficult nights they had experienced ever since their trip began. They hadn't experienced breathlessness like this before. Anurita, who always enjoys sound sleep, irrespective of where her stop is (tent, rock or a five-star bed!), couldn't boast of uninterrupted sleep in the night gone. It was strange how they felt suffocated in the middle of the night and even exchanged the hows and whys of it all. The morning was welcome and life was brighter. The sun shone and some birds hovered around. The stillness of the dead night was replaced with enthusiasm in welcoming the rest of the group. Outside the gate, and on the main road, were people mingling with one another. Most were locals, though a few were *yatris* pursuing their last-minute shopping before they headed towards the majestic mountain.

**Anurita:** Isn't it intriguing how we are suddenly feeling a lot better when just a few hours ago, in the middle of the night, we were so uncomfortable?

**Supriya:** That's nature marking its attendance in our lives.

**Anurita:** You enjoyed good health all along the way…do you feel you should have completed the *parikrama*?

**Supriya:** No, not quite. I wasn't quite as driven for the *parikrama,* though I must admit I enjoyed the beauty as well as the experience of trekking up a mountain. The climb back downward though seemed long and demanding, perhaps because one assumes that coming down is always easy! But looking back, I feel good that I did it.

**Anurita:** I'm waiting to hear stories our group will come armed with. The steep climb, horseback climb, oohs and the aahs, life-altering experiences—there'll be so much they would have gone through in this one and half days we weren't together. Our bus ride is going to be full of energy flowing across the seats and, well, we could expect a mini celebration of some sort along the way.

While Anurita was prone to thinking of pastries and sumptuous delights that follow celebration in cities, it was going to be a while before they could have that kind of a party to celebrate this feat in the mountains.

Kuldeep, Satpal and Anand stood near the gate, awaiting to board the bus, and looking forward to greet the trekkers. They did not have to wait too long.

For the trekkers, in about two hours the path began to level, and there in the distance, they could see their yaks and horses, waiting for them, for some reason. They reached that spot in

15 minutes, and to their surprise, found Mauley there. It was over. They had reached Darchen, and the bus would be coming along shortly to pick them up, along with the rest of the group. It was easy that day, and honestly, rather enjoyable.

Mauley informed them that when they were negotiating the Dolma La Pass the previous day, a 45-year-old Indian male suffered a heart attack and lost his life, somewhere near Gauri Kund. They were stumped; not knowing what else to do they hugged each other, shook hands, thanked the heavens for its blessings, and waited in quiet disbelief for the bus. I, of disinclination-towards-explaining-emotions fame, would rather narrate a Zen *Koan* here:

> Zen Master Ikkyu had always been quick in his thinking. This quickness often came in handy when he got in trouble as a young monk. On one such occasion, Ikkyu accidentally dropped his master's teacup, breaking it into many pieces.
>
> It was a serious problem, because the teacup was his master's favourite. It was a rare treasure; a beautifully handcrafted heirloom, wrought from precious material. Of all the master's possessions, it was probably the one thing he cherished the most—and now it was hopelessly smashed!
>
> Ikkyu felt guilty, but before he could formulate a plan to get away, he heard footsteps approaching. He swept the broken pieces together and, blocking them from view with his robe, turned to face the door just as the master entered.
>
> When they were within speaking distance, young Ikkyu asked, 'Master, why must people die?'
>
> The master replied, 'It is perfectly natural. Everything in the world experiences both life and death.'
>
> 'Everything?'

'Everything.'

'So it is not something we should feel upset about?'

'Definitely not. When its time has come every person and everything must go.'

'Master,' said little Ikkyu, shifting his robe aside to reveal the broken pieces, 'it was time for your cup to go. . . .'

The cup of life of this group was brimming with the epic experience. The moments they had spent on the mountain, lake and land, were going to be etched meaningfully in their memories forever. The aching muscles meant they had felt the earth beneath their feet, the breathlessness meant they were one with the surrounding energies, their sun-tanned faces meant they were connected to the heavenly orbs, their joyfulness meant they had lived!

They boarded the bus and did almost the entire journey to the point where the Land Cruisers were waiting, in deep thought, watching the sea of nature and humanity quivering outside in the bright sun. Perhaps the question agitating a majority of them was whether they would ever get the opportunity to return to the eternal mountain and the ethereal lake. There was palpable energy in each of the 14 group members that usually comes with the knowledge of having achieved something they never quite imagined. Anita and Anurita began to see the book form now, what with enriching experiences, some extreme weather conditions and also plentiful joy that they were brimming with. Anurita made a few musings and observations in anticipation of seeing the trekkers back, victorious and vibrant with energy. With no particular line of thought, it was more to put a stamp on the spirit of writing that Anita and she had decided to undertake in the near future.

Her little red diary read thus:

* The only things warmer than woollens and brighter than sunny climes is the joy of sharing on a trek. No calculations, no bargains, just readiness on offer.
* Taking a flight to reach destinations is a ticket to organised travel. However, there is nothing that can organise you and your life better than a ticket you allow your spirit to take amid nature.
* The lap of luxury is addictive but the lap of nature unforgettable.
* Before embarking on a trek, you're advised to visit a doctor and carry medicines in case of an emergency. After a trip to the mountains, you figure the best medicine is nature.
* Travel gets you to meet all sorts—from the grumpy to the smiling, the tough and weighty to those who take you lightly; it's a crash course in people management where you take the test and your degree comes instantly.
* When intentions are noble, you find help from different corners. In the face of opposition, the strong become helpful, the difficult warm up.
* A cycle is a companion that divorces fatigue to marry fitness.

On reaching their Land Cruisers parked about an hour away from Darchen, in almost a thin whisper, like the sound of an impetuous breeze ruffling the trees (well, it almost seemed like that after the *parikrama*), Harsh laid down their plan for the next three days.

**Harsh:** Today we camp outdoors at Paryang, tomorrow indoors at Nyalam, and the next day we drive to Kathmandu.

The group was silent and sizing Harsh with a deep sense of fulfilment.

> **Harsh:** We have very little time left to breathe in nature, before we get back to work, home and routine.

The group still silent, continued to size Harsh with a deep sense of fulfilment.

> **Harsh:** Fine then, Paryang it is. Are you guys sleeping with open eyes or what?
>
> **Anita:** Why do I feel the sudden urge to be bathed, cleaned, shampooed, tooth brushed, moisturised, you know the works? I merely ask to start a conversation.
>
> **Guarav:** Why do I feel that we can go straight to Nyalam today itself? It will not take us more than seven hours.
>
> **Kumaril:** That is a brilliant idea!
>
> **Gaurav:** I believe it is customary in good society to say thank you on being the subject of a compliment, so thank you.
>
> **Group:** Can we Harsh? Can we? Please, please, please?

Harsh did a quick consultation with Mauley and the drivers and returned, face beaming, to inform the group that their wishes were about to materialise. There were roars of approving laughter and instant endorsements. It took them about five hours to reach Nyalam, not only because the drivers drove as though mad dogs were let loose behind them, but also because they refused to be gentle on the utterly-broken-to-the-point-of-being-uncyclable roads of Saga.

After crossing Saga, when they stopped for lunch at a tiny motel, they somehow found comfort even in the lack of pomp. On that faultless day, Atul decided to humour himself and his camera with close-ups of the cyclists, rugged-tanned-bearded-serene look and all. They each posed with a debonair smile on their face, one that intimates its audience of complete appreciation of whatever was happening around in their life and times. They reached Nyalam as the sun settled in its lair, announcing that the unmistakable spread of orange and crimson twilight shall soon be followed by a starry-starry night. This time around, they stayed at a dharamshala at Nyalam, with very basic to almost nil amenities. There were three rooms, and they stayed five/four to a room. The women preferred to stay together in a room; they were anyway longing to catch up on some girlie chats. The loos were broken, the rooms were lived in, the linen had the smell of a thousand unbathed humans. . .but the group was happy. Nothing seemed to affect them anymore, with the intensity that it would have, in their earlier avatars. As they began to settle in their respective rooms, Atul called out.

**Atul:** Is this state of half silence and inactivity to remain permanent, or are any of you in a mood to elevate and amuse yourself with some hot drinks and junk food?

**Swati:** Have you seen the loos? Not that it matters anymore.

**Anurita:** The only thing that matters is we shall soon get to bathe! And, fun food soon after would be icing on the cake!

**Gaurav:** Atul, whatever put that extraordinary idea in your head, I am in.

**Supriya:** Did I hear someone say junk food? You have my attention and my appetite.

**Anita:** Supriya, with not an ounce of fat on you, you wouldn't know the first thing about junk food!

They continued chatting, laughing over silly jokes, and recounting cycling and trekking experiences over peanuts, cookies and other deep fried and enormously fatty stuff along with soup till late in the night, as if bed and breakfast were a long, long way off.

Trek done and *parikrama* through, some of the group members began dreaming of Nepal and all the restaurant hopping or shopping they could do there. Back to civilisation, they had enough to look forward to. The days in those tents would be a lasting memory but for now, they were geared up to embrace what was approaching. And that included a long drive the next day accompanied with some tuck, lots of chatter, some philosophising and looking back with loads of interesting episodes to share with family and friends once back in their nests.

The next morning, they started for Kathmandu sharp at 8 am. Some people are born to get up early, some achieve this difficult feat through years of practice and some have early mornings thrust on them. The cyclists belonged to the first category, Swati and Supriya had risen to the second, but Anita, Anurita and Kuldeep belonged to the hugely popular and prosperous third category. However, with all their thoughts focused on the future, that is a scenic ride ahead through the mountains of Tibet and Nepal teeming with waterfalls, they were always ready on time.

# 21

***QUIDDITY***

***Kwi-diti***

*(noun) Origin: Latin*

*Whatever makes something the type that it is; the essence of something*

**DAY FOURTEEN:** *Nyalam to Nagarkot, Nepal*

**DAY FIFTEEN:** *Nagarkot to Kathmandu*

For those of you who've got used to the timetable presentation or here-is-how-the-day-looks-like at the start of each day, there's a digression here. Anita being a tiny specimen of humanity identifies very well with the character Asterix in the French comic series *Asterix and Obelix*. The manner in which the underdogs led by the puny Asterix stand up to the taller and bigger forces, to her, is nothing short of a victory over limitations. She loves these comics to the extent that her mind is constantly cataloguing people she knows, meets, and is friends or relatives with, into *Asterix*-like situations and giving them the nomenclature to go with it. During my eavesdropping sessions, I had once too often listened on as she would categorise every passer-by thus. Later, I heard this hilarious recount by Swati, of her doing the same with the group.

Apparently, on the last night at Nyalam, as the group plopped around their tuck in an aesthetic relaxation, she ventured to characterise the group and met with no resistance, in fact, they joined her. No surprise there!

**Anita:** After so many days of togetherness and provocation, I am compelled to pause and indulge in naming us *Asterix* comics style.

**Sanjeeta:** We somehow feel as if we have fallen from heaven afresh and anew, so it anyway calls for *de novo* baptism.

**Gaurav:** Go ahead. Name us, but with reasoning.

**Anita:** Gaurav, you are *Lawsome* for keeping watch and ward and for being the time-keeper to the world, the nation and the group.

**Supriya:** You are spot on!

**Anita:** Not so soon, Supriya. You are *Jollymaximus* for no reason other than a nursery rhyme that goes—Supriya has a dog for a pet, with fleece as black as a crow, and everywhere that Jolly goes, Supriya is sure to go!

**Sanjeeta:** Oh, this is too fascinating! So how would you name someone who is extraordinarily seasoned in his approach to life and times?

**Anita:** You mean Haresh? He is *Quietlymatura.* Nothing seems to ruffle him, appal him, or bother him enough for even the hint of an irritation to alight on the surface.

**Haresh:** One evolves as the years roll on. In my youth I have been peevish.

**Kumaril:** All those who consider themselves of advanced age may consult the horsemen of Tibet fame for age verification!

**Sanjeeta:** Kumaril, it is your turn now.

**Anita:** He is entitled to consideration and respect as a story-teller, hence I have named him *Anecdotix.*

**Anurita:** Allow me to name Sanjeeta.

**Sanjeeta:** Of course. Tell me. Tell me!

**Anurita:** For being the mainspring of energy and excitement, I name you, Sanjeeta, *Buoyantix*.

**Sanjeeta:** I love that! What about Harsh?

**Anita:** *Fulliauotomatix* for his HOWness.

**Harsh:** Ha ha. And Atul?

**Anurita:** My turn. Atul is *Wittyholix* for his wisecracks.

**Atul**: Hmm. Why do I smell a dose of methylated spirit in my name?

**Anurita:** Because such wit is normally expected from one who is in the throes of intoxication.

**Satpal:** If that is the case, then please name Rajiv for his love interest.

**Rajiv:** What love interest? How come such a crucial piece of information is hidden from me?

**Satpal:** Don't go overboard. It's your camera I am talking about.

**Anita:** That is why he is *Photographix*.

**Rajiv:** I like that. That is a name for keepsake. What would you name yourself?

**Atul:** Let me guess. It should be *Horsemania*. Need I explain why?

**Anita:** On the dot!

**Gaurav:** What about Anand?

**Anurita:** *Catalytix* for being the inspiration of the group despite his history of paraplegia.

**Anita:** And Satpal is best described as *Discountfix*.

**Satpal:** (Grinning from ear to ear) The shopkeepers' union would hunt me down, if only they knew!

**Kuldeep:** I am still a waiting to be christened.

**Anita:** You are *Linguistix* for being fluent in all languages unknown to the group, and Anurita you are *Jewelpix* for your unmatched ability to spot colourful stones on the sandy beaches of Lake Manasarovar.

**Anurita:** Ah! That day spent on the Lake was wonderful indeed!

**Swati:** Since I am the last one to be Asterixed, I expect a unique one.

**Anita:** You, my lady, are *Loominous* for showing us the way.

**Kuldeep:** Way to what?

**Anita:** (Winking) To a place where no man has been before!

Alright, let's un-digress and go back to where we belong. Nagarkot was not on the itinerary; it was merely an unintended but welcome side-effect of the lasting impression of Tibet on the group that continued to spill over en route to Nepal. Tibet had provided a perfect example in three-dimension of how quickly you can get transported from the hurry and scurry of daily life to a place of joy and tranquillity. The group was not about to change their status (as they say on social media) so soon.

Gauging the mood of the group, it was Mauley who suggested in his cutely old-fashioned manner, 'Respectable sirs and madams, since we will be arriving a day earlier than scheduled at Kathmandu, would you like to consider detouring to Nagarkot? There is a charming resort on the hilltop there. You may like to relax there for a day. I am only suggesting, it is your call.'

Of course, they wanted to detour. It was as if Mauley had read their minds with uncanny exactitude. So, the detour was favoured and welcomed with much noise and clumsy dancing on a rattling bus.

A relaxed and joyful-for-no-reason mind is not in the best season for literary effort. However, at the lunch place, Anita and Anurita did discuss in rather rapid tones, within my hearing distance, the details of how they would present this part of their trip. To any outsider overhearing their excited voices, it would be suggestive of a spirited attempt at verbally assaulting someone, but for me, being used to and in love with their eager manner, it made a great deal of sense.

After enduring a five-hour ride from Nyalam interspersed with the usual checkpoints manned by the standard fierce men in cop clothes, and a very precarious uphill drive on a very pleasant hill, they reached the hilltop resort in Nagarkot. An area full of thickly forested hills of pine trees, Nagarkot is on the northern side of the Kathmandu Valley and is famous for the magnificent views it affords of the Himalayas. Eight of the 13 Himalayan ranges of Nepal—Annapurna range, Manaslu range, Ganesh Himal range, Langtang range, Jugal range, Rolwaling range, Mahalangur range (Everest range) and Numbur range—can be viewed from here on a clear day. From the resort, through the mist, manicured gardens and lush greenery, the entire expanse of the Kathmandu valley could also be seen. As soon as they reached, the delicate balance that they had maintained so far, between to-be (clean) or not-to-be (clean) tipped increasingly in favour of the former.

**Harsh:** Guys, I am going to get a little busy now in having a much-needed, hot-water bath.

**Kumaril:** Who did you think would interrupt? We shall all be busy in the same delightful activity.

**Rajiv:** And after the bath, I plan to lose myself to the outdoors.

**Anita:** Ah for a bath! It suddenly feels as if a huge weight has been lifted off my mind.

**Atul:** Some minds are not constructed to bear great weights, I should imagine.

**Anita:** (Targeting a murderous stare at Atul) Define the 'some'! Right now!

**Atul:** I wasn't talking of your mind. No, never. *Marna hai kya* (Do I want to die)!

**Supriya:** Hmm. War and peace!

**Anurita:** Manasarovar was a heavenly experience but this is going to be like visiting the heaven, staying there for a bit, and emerging like fairies who would then treat themselves to some soupy delights and savoury bitings.

**Kuldeep:** Ha ha, food and you can't part.

**Anurita:** Good food, you mean! And the experience gets doubly amazing when you are at a venue like this. A book in hand, some exciting delights in a plate and a hot drink besides, overlooking this beautiful landscape should be great. But first things first. Am now off for the bath of my life!

A good deal of mixed activity followed. All 14 indulged in the much-awaited bath in instalments and wrestled with the dirt and grime of over 10 days. But since there were two to a room, at least half of them flitted to and fro—some taking pictures from the garden, some hanging out in the balcony attached to their rooms, some savouring a cup of tea in the resort restaurant, few frantically searching for clean clothes in their bulging bags (bulging due to the haphazard packing). But when they finally emerged in the outdoor restaurant of the resort, in salutary forms, they looked at each other in utter disbelief. The grubby faces had magically disappeared to reveal polished, clean people, you know the kind that attend office on time and beam over files and work as though a special breed handcrafted by God! I knew though, it wasn't the bath, but the bright lustre on faces and the sparkle in demeanour that came from deep within.

Fresh from a trek that wasn't child's play, and yet, the group didn't want to stay indoors in the comforts of the hotel; instead, they began planning to take a walk around. Didn't they want to sleep? Or simply relax and unwind watching a film on television? Or perhaps reply to the hundreds of messages on their phones from near and dear ones across the nearly two-week break from civilisation? No, not at all. While a few excused themselves for a siesta they knew they most deserved, some of the enthusiastic ones set out for a walk around the hotel. A local standing outside the hotel gate began guiding them on the little bylanes around or the route they could take for a great walk in the scenic environs.

**Anurita:** I wouldn't mind just sitting aimlessly on one of these wayside rocks that overlook the landscape and stare into nothingness.

**Haresh:** Since you have the camera hung around your neck, would you not want to photograph the surroundings, Kuldeep?

**Kuldeep:** Oh yes, I am always ready to take pictures.

**Anurita:** Especially when the pictures have me, right? Ha ha....

The group laughed on little jokes they cracked on and with each other. That was how they had kick-started their day, every day, during the trek. The campsites are left with flooding memories of this group that was, to us cycles, unforgettable and one of a kind. While some in the group spoke a good deal, there were those who were fairly quiet in disposition. But what I liked most was that each one, at some point, was bonding with another over different things. Sometimes breakfast and coffee, often photography, and almost always on little notes to stay charged and healthy in unfavourable weather conditions. Of course, all this was interspersed with different experiences from their lives, their learnings and lessons. That positive streak and ability to laugh at themselves is what kept the group in good cheer. If one was down and out, the other would surround to inject energy and enthusiasm. That inner calm perhaps reflected on their bright faces that had, post the grand bath, become brighter.

Every time I feel limited when expressing, a Zen *Koan* comes in handy, as you may have observed.

> Fa-yen, a Chinese Zen teacher, overheard four monks arguing about subjectivity and objectivity.
>
> He joined them and said, 'There is a big stone. Do you consider it to be inside or outside your mind?'
>
> One of the monks replied, 'From the Buddhist viewpoint everything is an objectification of mind, so I would say that the stone is inside my mind.'
>
> 'Your head must feel very heavy,' observed Fa-yen, 'if you are carrying around a stone like that in your mind.'

Applying too much of intellect, reasoning and logic often leads to stones in the mind. But here was a group that seemed to have acquired a taste of life beyond all that. They felt different somehow. There were no stones in the mind—only a mountain and a lake, both of which felt like a blessing. They were happy, just plain and simple happy.

After spending a fruitful day and night at Nagarkot, on Day Fifteen, the group boarded the bus for the last time to go to Kathmandu, back to Hotel Marshyangdi.

The day was hectic. The women went to the shopping streets, looking for nothing in particular, but wanting everything they saw. The men followed suit. It was in this shopping trip that Anita bought some of the books on Tibet that are referred to here. Besides her, others who shopped on that Nepal street, picked up local handicrafts, fabric and pickles, even some junk jewellery. Where there are women, it is the norm. But if you find men buying jewellery, know that they had orders from the higher court to bring back beautiful somethings along with beautiful memories!

Kuldeep and Anurita enjoyed walking into the little cafes dotting the street. While at one point they stopped to check out Pilgrims Book House that had caught fire and was burnt to ashes, there was another bookstore that looked inviting due to the postcards that hung right outside its door—like airy curtains that play hide and seek with the room they guard and the world beyond it.

**Kuldeep:** Do you not want to pick up anything?

**Anurita:** May be a couple of books for sure. But, first things first. I'd like catching up on a pastry in that café across.

**Haresh:** Alright, let me treat you to this one! A toast to sweet times together, in years to come.

Later that evening, Harsh, Gaurav and Atul got into the act of returning tentage, equipment, and us cycles back to Explore Himalayas. When we were being placed in our warehouse, I overheard the three discussing that they were to leave for India the next day. Silently, we cycles bid them farewell. We had grown so fond of them, and they of us. It was tough to part and yet part we had to. Everything and everyone has a time and slot in your life and they exit when the time is up. Nothing quite happens by chance, it is designed to be a certain way. We were perhaps fated for this wonderful journey with cyclists and the Support Group who had benevolent hearts and often took interest in how we fared. Inspired by Dattatreya, I have become a learner in my daily life. From the group I have learnt that you do not just visit nature, you be in the moment in it, you listen to it, you let it enter your being and you absorb it. I learnt that there is a child in everyone, and at any stage in life when you become the child, you become yourself, joyful for no reason under the sun, and you take the first step to enlightenment. You do not have to go searching for happiness; you just have to dissolve in it. And finally, that in each precious breath we take, there is an entire universe desiring that we remain in awareness, blissfulness and calmness.

*Nestled in enchanting environs, the hotel in Nagarkot, Nepal, was a 'gift' of sorts*
*Photo credit: Rajiv Popli*

*Our world has turned pleasantly upside down*
*Photo credit: Satpal Singh Chhabda*

# 22

## *DENOUEMENT*

***Dei-nu-mei***

*(noun) Origin: French*

*The final part of something, such as a book, a play, or a series of events; the resolution of a narrative*

Some people are nice, and some not so nice. But surely that is something that friends and relatives of such people can decide for themselves based on a series of good, bad and ugly experiences. But, it's easy to just feel the ride while on the saddle of a cycle and know in the deepest recesses that the cycle is good, and that you feel comfortable on it, enough to submit several moments of your life unconditionally to it. With nature too, it is just the same. Just a whiff of fresh air or the scent of flowers blossoming in the crannies of rocks, or the sight and sound of a gushing stream, or the vicinity of an ancient mountain or even the falling of raindrops on a tin roof, is like instant caffeine. It energises. It gives life a perspective. It shows where you belong in the majestic universe—you belong here and now!

I cannot imagine a better way of ending this narration than with a few *Koans*. These extraordinarily short and simple Zen stories imitate our extraordinarily short but complicated lives.

> A little boy was late getting home one day. When he finally showed up, his worried mother asked, 'Where have you been?'
>
> The little boy explained, 'I stopped to help a friend whose bicycle had broken down.'

'But you don't know how to fix a bicycle,' his mother said.

'That's true,' replied the little boy. 'But I stopped to be with him while he cried.'

In this group of 14, most of them were neither expert cyclists nor sturdy trekkers. Yet the 'withness' that you see in this *Koan* is the kind of 'withness' with nature and with each other that they experienced in this trip.

A priest was in charge of the garden within a famous Zen temple. He had been given the job because he loved the flowers, shrubs and trees. Next to the temple there was another smaller temple, where lived a very old Zen master. One day, when the priest was expecting some special guest, he took extra care in tending to the garden. He pulled out the weeds, trimmed the shrubs, combed the mosses, and spent a long time meticulously raking up and carefully arranging all the dry leaves. As he worked, the old master watched him with interest from across the wall that separated the temples.

When he finished, the priest stood back to admire his work. 'Isn't it beautiful?' he called out to the old master. 'Yes,' replied the old master, 'but there is something missing. Help me over this wall and I'll put it right for you.'

After hesitating, the priest lifted the old fellow over and set him down. Slowly, the master walked to the tree near the centre of the garden, grabbed it by the trunk and shook it. Leaves fell in showers all over the garden. 'There,' said the old man, 'you can put me back now.'

Nature is perfect, there is nothing to add, nothing to delete and Tibet is a living example of this. The 14 people in this story may seem to be full of imperfections if you were to examine them under a microscope. But they tried not only to see but also accept each other and their surroundings just the way it were, imperfections and all, and ended up bonding with all of it for life. Finding beauty in imperfection is the closest we will ever get to perfection!

And finally, I end with my story. It is *my* story because it echoes my philosophy of life. This is a story from the Taoist tradition. Tao means 'the way' or 'the path', and Taoism professes doing things the simple and natural way or 'doing by not doing'. We bicycles are adept at going with the flow; it is humans that struggle against it. But deep in the mountains, at elevations above 14,000 feet, even if through the medium of skilfully negotiating drivers and lack of basic amenities, I have this strange feeling that my 14 favourite people on earth too learnt to go with the flow.

> An old man accidentally fell into the river rapids leading to a high and dangerous waterfall. Onlookers feared for his life. Miraculously, he came out alive and unharmed downstream at the bottom of the falls.
>
> People asked him how he managed to survive.
>
> 'I accommodated myself to the water, not the water to me. Without thinking, I allowed myself to be shaped by it. Plunging into the swirl, I came out with the swirl. This is how I survived.'

What do you do when you are sitting next to a lake as ethereal as Manasarovar or standing face-to-face with the eternal mountain, Mount Kailash? You listen to the gentle breeze, you watch the tiny playful waves on the surface of the lake, you feel the energy of the mountain seep within you, you absorb it all, in silence, in thought or thoughtlessness, you feel at ease and complete, you stop struggling against anything and everything. Just this silence within, and the complete absence of struggle, may perhaps be the most spiritual thing you might ever do. This is really the way for much to happen to you—both inside and outside. Because when you stop, look around and be with the moment, this life becomes the gift it was meant to be!

Goodbye, dear friends, philosophers and riders! Until we meet again as something, somewhere, sometime. . .in this wonderful thing called life. It has indeed been quite a journey!

*The purpose of a fish trap is to catch fish,*
*And when the fish are caught, the trap is forgotten.*

*The purpose of a rabbit snare is to catch rabbits.*
*When the rabbits are caught, the snare is forgotten.*

*The purpose of words is to convey ideas.*
*When the ideas are grasped, the words are forgotten.*

*Where can I find a man who has forgotten words?*
*He is the one I would like to talk to.*

**Chuang-Tsu**

## *EPILOGUE*

### *Epee-log*

*(noun) Origin: French, Latin and Greek*

*A final section or speech or expression after the main part of the book is over*

*Beyond vision and sound*
*Beyond meanings*
*Beyond pleasure and pain*
*Beyond feelings*
*In the realm of consciousness*
*Where attachments cease*
*I have created my own*
*Stillness and peace*
*I come from the mountains*
*The mountains live in me*
*I grow from the lakes*
*The lakes flow from me*
*Spring and autumn*
*From me arrive*
*I spring from them*
*In them I thrive*
*Stone and water*
*Are born in my thoughts*
*They have crafted me*
*They connect my dots*
*Inside and outside*
*All is complete*
*Nothing to add*
*Nothing to delete.*

# The Schedule

| Day | Schedule | Km | Altitude in mts | Oxygen (Percentage of that at sea level) | Number of km Cycled/Trekked |
|---|---|---|---|---|---|
| **One** | Arrive at Kathmandu by air from Delhi | | | | |
| **Two** | Cross border at Kodari and proceed to Nyalam by bus | 162 km to Kodari<br>35 km from border to Nyalam | 3,800 | 60 | – |
| **Three** | Nyalam—rest day for acclimatisation | | 3,800 | 62 | – |
| **Four** | Nyalam to Peikutso campsite | 142 | 4,430 | 50 at Nyalam Pass | 90 cycled |
| **Five** | Peikutso to Saga campsite by road | 130 | 4580 | 56 | No cycling |
| **Six** | Saga to Dongba campsite | 136 | 4,700 | 54 | 32 cycled |

| Day | Schedule | Km | Altitude in mts | Oxygen (Percentage of that at sea level) | Number of km Cycled/Trekked |
|---|---|---|---|---|---|
| **Seven** | Dongba to Paryang campsite | 139 | 4,500 | 56 | 92 cycled |
| **Eight** | Paryang to Mayumula campsite | 116 | 4,670 | 54 (50 at Mayumula Pass) | 49 cycled |
| **Nine** | Mayumula to Horse-shoe point before Lake Manasarovar;<br>Horse-shoe point to shore of Lake Manasarovar;<br>Camp at shore of the Lake | 37<br>80 | 4,560 | 55 | 37 cycled<br>By bus |
| **Ten** | Manasarovar to Darchen | 40 | 4,575 | 55 | By bus |
| **Eleven** | Parikrama: From Yam Dwaar (near Darchen) to Dirapukh | 18 | 5,150 | 52 | Trekked |

| Day | Schedule | Km | Altitude in mts | Oxygen (Percentage of that at sea level) | Number of km Cycled/Trekked |
|---|---|---|---|---|---|
| **Twelve** | Parikrama: Dirapukh to Zutulpukh | 22 | 4,760 | 54 (47 at Dolma Pass) | Trekked |
| **Thirteen** | Parikrama: Zutulpukh to Darchen | 12 | 4,575 | 55 | Trekked |
| | Darchen to Nyalam | 550 | 3,800 | 60 | By Land Cruisers |
| **Fourteen** | Nyalam to Nagarkot, Nepal | 150 | 4,500 | 56 | By Land Cruisers upto the China-Nepal border followed by bus in Nepal |
| **Fifteen** | Nagarkot to Kathmandu | | | | By Bus |
| | | **TOTAL** | | | 300 km cycling; 52 km trekking |

# Glossary

---

*LAGOM*

***Lay-gaum***

*(adj) Origin: Swedish*

*Just right; neither too much nor too little; adequate*

---

**ABC:** Ahmedabad Bicycling Club.

**Adi Sankaracharaya:** A monk and philosopher in the 8th century AD. He is known to be the first person to consolidate the Advaita thought, and establish the doctrine of Hinduism by consolidating the main currents of thought.

**Advaita:** This is the philosophy that establishes that there is but one reality in the universe, that of the Supreme consciousness, and that all other facets of reality are but a part of that whole, including the individual soul. It is loosely termed as non-duality.

**Avalokiteshwara:** The 'Lord who looks down' is a Bodhisattva who manifests all of Buddha's compassion. The three bodhisattvas—Avalokiteshwara, Manjushree and Vajrapani—are the earliest representations of protective bodhisattvas who surround the Buddha.

**Avatar:** The human or animal manifestation of a Hindu god on earth; this term is also used to represent someone who represents a particular quality or type.

**AWOL:** Absent Without Official Leave.

**Baldev:** Also known as 'Balarama', an Indian God of agriculture, generally depicted as carrying a plough on his shoulders.

**Bodhisattva:** A person who motivated by sheer compassion desires to attain Buddhahood for the benefit of sentient beings.

**Bollywood:** The Hindi film industry in Mumbai is popularly known as Bollywood.

**Bon:** A religion followed in Tibet from around 11th century AD. It describes itself as different from Buddhism, yet draws some tenets from it.

**Chakra:** An energy node or point in our subtle bodies that is a channel for the universal energy to flow in. Believed as such in Buddhism, Hinduism and Jainism.

**Chitrakoot:** An area in the Satna district of the province of Madhya Pradesh in India, where it is believed that Lord Ram spent 14 years of exile in.

**Dal:** Lentils.

**Dattatreya:** Considered a deity who came on earth as an incarnation of the Trinity—Brahma, Vishnu and Shiva—he is revered as Adi Guru or First Teacher. It is believed that his original footprints can be found in Mount Girnar in Gujarat. He believed and taught that there is something that we can learn from everyone and everything that surrounds us.

**Dharamshala:** A rest house specially created for pilgrims.

**Diamox:** When climbing above heights of 10,000 feet/3,048 metres, this drug can be very helpful in mitigating the signs of altitude sickness such as headache, dizziness, nausea, tiredness, breathlessness, etc. The chemical composition is Acetazolamide. In the Kailash Manasarovar trek, it is advisable to take this in the required dosage.

**Dolma La:** This is a mountain Pass and is the highest point in the Kailash *Parikrama* and entails the toughest part of the trek. It is at a height of 19,500 feet and the north-eastern face of Mount Kailash is clearly visible from here.

**Gauri Kund:** This turquoise green water body can be seen at the bottom as soon as you cross Dolma La, and look down the mountainside. It is also known as Lake of Compassion and is situated at 5,608 metres.

**Gurudwara:** Place of worship for people who follow Sikhism.

**Idli:** A cake of fermented lentils and rice, popularly eaten for breakfast in South India.

**Jai ho:** Let victory be ours.

**Kaka:** Normally a word used for father's younger brother, it is also used to address an aged person, a staffer who works for you, or someone you don't know the name of but want to call out to. Quite like the way the term '*bhaiya*' is used across India to address someone you don't know but want to address.

**Khakhra:** Thin breads, almost like a thin cracker, these are generally made of oil and wheat flour, and is a popular snack in Gujarat.

**Khichdi:** Indian preparation made from rice and lentils; considered to be very healthy and easy on the stomach.

**Koan:** In Zen Buddhism, very tiny stories called Koans are used to provoke enlightenment. These are anecdotal or in the form of riddles. The listener is expected to interpret it in accordance with his level of enlightenment. Koans demonstrate to some extent the inadequacy of logic and reasoning.

**Kora:** A Tibetan word that refers to both, the circumambulation around a pilgrimage site and to the entire experience of a pilgrimage.

**Kundalini:** Latent energy, female in character, located at the base of the spine.

**Manali-Leh-Khardungla:** This is a scenic and tough route for cycling, starting from Manali in Himachal Pradesh and going to Khardung Pass in the Ladakh region of Jammu and Kashmir that at 5,602 metres is the highest motorable road in the world.

**Mandala:** A spiritually symbolic or metaphysical representation of the cosmos in Hinduism and Buddhism. It is also used as an aid to meditation.

**Mandana Mishra:** A Hindu philosopher from the 8th century AD who was a staunch follower of the Karma Mimansa (with focus on rituals) school of thought, before he met Adi Sankaracharya. After the famous debate with Sankaracharya, Mandana became his disciple and propagated the Advaita (with focus on knowledge of self and spirituality) philosophy.

**Manjushree:** A bodhisattva meaning 'Gentle Glory', and is associated with the manifestation of all of Buddha's wisdom. The three bodhisattvas, Avalokiteshwara, Manjushree and Vajrapani, are the earliest representations of protective bodhisattvas who surround the Buddha.

**Meghdoot:** Around the 5th century AD, there lived somewhere in North India as per speculation, a classical Sanskrit writer, Kalidasa. Meghdoot is one of his most famous works. It is a composition of 111 Sanskrit verses and is the story of a *yaksha* (benevolent nature spirits who take care of the nature's hidden bounties) exiled to central India, yearning for his wife who lives at Alaka on Mount Kailash. He convinces a passing cloud to take his message to his wife, by giving vivid descriptions of the scenic beauty that the cloud will come across on its way to Alaka.

**Mela:** Funfair that has joy rides, food and game stalls, and related activities.

**Milarepa:** Considered Tibet's most famous and highly revered yogi and poet who lived from 1052–1135 AD.

**Naka:** Checkposts at regular intervals on highways.

**Nirvana:** A term more commonly used in Buddhism to represent salvation or liberation from the cycle of birth and death.

**Parikrama:** Hindi term for circumambulation.

**Parvat:** Mountain in Hindi.

**Parvati:** The Indian Goddess of love, power, fertility and strength, considered as Mother Goddess in Hinduism, she is the wife of Lord Shiva.

**Past life regression:** A technique that uses hypnosis to make the subject recover memories of past life and/or incarnations.

**Pilgrims Book House:** A popular book shop in Nepal that was destroyed in a fire in 2013.

**Reinhold Messner:** Born in 1944, he is an acclaimed mountaineer from Italy. He and Habeler were the first to climb Mount Everest without supplemental oxygen in 1978. In 1986, Reinhold became the first mountaineer ever to have climbed all 14 peaks that are eight-thousanders, that is, mountains with a height of more than 8,000 metres. In 2004, at the age of 60, he completed a 2,000 km expedition through the Gobi Desert. He has written over 60 books. He is fairly unstoppable.

**Roti:** Indian flatbread made of wheat flour.

**Sachin Tendulkar:** Former Indian cricketer and captain of the Indian team, his achievements in international cricket are the stuff that legends are made of.

**Shackleton:** (1874–1922) Sir Ernest Shackleton was a British explorer who was rediscovered in late 20th century as the man who led his entire team on the broken ship *Endurance* to survival through several months of facing extreme circumstances.

**Shambhala:** It is a mythical kingdom according to Tibetan Buddhist texts with which several teaching and healing practices are associated. Even the Hindu text, *Vishnu Purana,* mentions the name of a village called Shambhala, where it is predicted that the tenth and last reincarnation of Lord Vishnu, that is Kalki, will take birth, and usher in a golden period.

**Shivling:** Ling means symbol or mark, and Shivling is the representation of Lord Shiva, or the form in which he is worshipped in most temples.

**Shiva:** The Hindu Trinity of major gods includes—Brahma the creator, Vishnu the sustainer and Shiva the transformer.

**Thanka:** A Tibetan Buddhist painting mostly done on silk cloth using vibrant vegetable colours. It generally depicts a Buddhist deity or a scene from Buddha's or a Bodhisattva's life or a Mandala.

**Tirthankara:** In Jainism, a person who has reached the highest level of enlightenment and creates a path for others to follow. Mahavira of the 6th century AD was the 24th and last Tirthankara.

**Ubhaya Bharati:** Wife of Mandana Mishra, and a very renowned scholar of Hindu philosophy, she gave a tough fight to Adi Sankaracharya in a debate where he was trying to establish the superiority of the philosophy of Advaita.

**Vajrapani:** This bodhisattva is meant to protect Buddha and manifests all of Buddha's powers. The three bodhisattvas, Avalokiteshwara, Manjushree and Vajrapani are the earliest representations of protective bodhisattvas who surround the Buddha.

**Yama:** The Hindu god of death.

**Yantra:** A Hindu mystical diagram typically drawn with nine interlocking triangles that radiate out from a central point. It is used as an aid for meditation.

**Yatra:** Journey or a pilgrimage.

**Yatri:** Traveller.

**Zen:** This is the Japanese school of Buddhism which focuses on mindfulness or being in the moment and inner peace, through meditation and inner intuition.

# Bibliography

---

***ASTERISM***

***As-turh-ism***

*(noun) Origin: Greek*

*Constellation or a group of stars*

---

Charles Allen, *A Mountain in Tibet*, Abacus, UK, 2013.

Charles Bell, *Religion of Tibet*, Indian edition, Motilal Banarsidass Publishers Private Limited, Delhi, 2000.

Colin Thubron, *To a Mountain in Tibet*, Harper Collins, 2012.

Deepak Chopra, *Synchrodestiny: Harnessing the Infinite Power of Coincidence to Create Miracles*, Rider, 2005.

Dawa Norbu, *Tibet, The Road Ahead*, Harper Collins Publishers India Pvt Ltd., 1997.

Mrityunjay, *Meghdoot: The Emissary of Sunderance*, Trafford Publishing, USA, 2012.

Pandit Rajmani Tigunait, *The Himalayan Masters: A Living Tradition*, Himalayan Institute, India, 2002.

Patrick French, *Tibet – A Personal History of a Lost Land*, Vintage Departures (A division of Random House Inc.) New York, 2002.

Robert M Pirsig, *Zen and the Art of Motorcycle Maintenance: An Inquiry into values*, Harper Collins, 1974.

Sam Van Schaik, *Tibet: A History*, Yale University Press, New Haven and London, 2011.

Shunryu Suzuki, *Zen Mind, Beginner's Mind*, Weatherhill, 1970.

Thrangu Rinpoche, *Rechungpa: A Biography of Milarepa's Disciple*, (translated by Peter Alan Roberts) Namo Buddha Publications, Glastonbury, 2002.

Thomas Laird, *The Story of Tibet: Conversations with the Dalai Lama*, Grove Press, New York, 2006.

Tsangnyon Heruka, *The Life of Milarepa*, (translated by Andrew Quintman) Penguin Books, 2010.

W.Y. Evan-Wentz, *Tibet's Great Yogi, Milarepa*, Oxford University Press, 2000.

## Websites Referred

Om Mani Padme Hum: http://www.sacred-texts.com/bud/tib/omph.htm

Taoist story: http://users.rider.edu/~suler/zenstory/zenframe.html https://en.wikipedia.org/wiki/Effects_of_high_altitude_on_humans

Tibet Environmental Watch—Reports—Archived: http://www.tew.org/archived/kailash.story.html

Zen Koan: A broken tea cup: http://zeninsights.com/category/koans/#

Zen Koan: Broken bicycle: https://philipchircop.wordpress.com/tag/bicycle/

Zen Koan: Five cyclists: http://www.willamette.edu/~mjaneba/cycling/Bike_Zen_Koan.html

Zen Koan: Inside and outside: http://www.katinkahesselink.net/tibet/zen-stories.html

Zen Koan: Judgment: http://www.arcane-archive.org/religion/buddhism/zen/bike-koan-1.php

Zen Koan: Master across the garden: http://users.rider.edu/~suler/zenstory/zenframe.html

Zen Koan: This too shall pass: http://zeninsights.com/category/koans/page/4/

## Poems

1. An Ode to an Expedition Cyclist—Anita Karwal
2. Epilogue—Anita Karwal

3. I am a Cycle—Anita Karwal
4. Lake Manasarovar—Anita Karwal
5. Lake Peiku Tso—Anita Karwal
6. Prologue—Anita Karwal
7. The Paryang Rain—Anita Karwal
8. World Within and Beyond—Anurita Rathore

# ACKNOWLEDGEMENTS

***NAMASTE***

***Nah-mus-tay***

*(Noun) Origin: Sanskrit*

*It is a form of greeting in India and some of its neighbouring countries where there is influence of Hinduism; it is in fact a reverential salutation and it means that my soul bows in honour of your soul*

It is an energising thought that there are people in this world who we can acknowledge for being a part of one of the most exquisite journeys of our lives.

There are a handful of people who made it possible to pen this book, and our thanks are surely in place for those. Members of the group, some who cycled and formed the premise, and those that did not cycle but lent their observations, a big thank you to each one. You own the book as much as you did the journey.

We are indebted to our publisher, Dipankar Mukherjee, whose enthusiasm and nod for the book sealed our smiles, and for sharing thoughts and suggestions that make this book a joyful ride.

It's good luck when one comes across calm, collected and cheerful editors. Thank you Indrani Ganguly, our editor, for further watering our desire to write.

Our first words find encouragement and appreciation in parents; they can never be thanked enough. Sudha and Madan Mohan Bhatnagar, nourished Anita's dreams and aspirations and guided them to fruition. Sanyukta and Bhupendravijay Singh Rathore are the strong foundation that shaped Anurita's thoughts and ideologies letting her believe everything is possible with intent and strong will—every nod and wish lit up paths. We thank them for their blessings, they are nothing short of divinity for us.

Atul, Anita's husband, her best friend and the perfect sounding board, and Janvi and Tanvi, their daughters, together form a terrific cheering team for Anita and somehow it has made all the difference. Kuldeep, Anurita's husband, is her backbone and buddy, pillar and punch bag; their daughter, Ankulanjana fuels her belief that life can indeed be magical. Thank you from the bottom of our hearts.

Mount Kailash and Lake Manasarovar have become a sublime presence in our lives, constantly goading us to imbibe their spirit, calmness and placidity within our recesses. We bow before you.